THE KINCORA SCANDAL

POLITICAL COVER-UP AND INTRIGUE IN NORTHERN IRELAND

CHRIS MOORE

FOREWORD BY CLIFFORD SMYTH

First published in 1996 by
Marino Books
An imprint of Mercier Press
16 Hume Street Dublin 2

Trade enquiries to Mercier Press
PO Box 5, 5 French Church Street,
Cork

© Chris Moore 1996
© Foreword Clifford Smyth 1996

ISBN 1 86023 029 6

10 9 8 7 6 5 4 3 2 1

A CIP record for this title is available from the British Library

Cover photos by Chris Moore, Derek Speirs/Report and Alan McCullough
Cover design by Bluett
Set by Richard Parfrey
Printed in Ireland by ColourBooks, Baldoyle Industrial Estate, Dublin 13

This book is sold subject to the condition that it shall not, by way of trade or otherwise, be lent, resold, hired out or otherwise circulated without the publisher's prior consent in any form of binding or cover other than that in which it is published and without a similar condition including this condition being imposed on the subsequent purchaser.

No part of this publication may be reproduced or transmitted in any form or by any means, electronic or mechanical, including photocopying, recording or any information or retrieval system, without the prior permission of the publisher in writing.

Contents

Acknowledgements	5
Author's Note	7
Foreword by Clifford Smyth	11
Prologue	15

Part I: For God and Ulster 1955-67
1	Faith House	21
2	Cell Becomes Tara	34

Part II: Ulster at the Crossroads 1968-71
3	What Kind of Ulster?	49
4	'Doomsday' is Nigh	58
5	'Our Heritage'	71
6	On the Fringes	80

Part III: Kincora 1958-71
7	A Home from Home	92
8	Enter the Beast	104

Part IV: Guns and Politics 1974-80
9	McGrath, Tara, Guns and the Man from the Ministry	116
10	Out of Africa	126
11	Shadow Politics	136

Part V: The Beginning of the End 1980-82
12	Day 1: Thursday 24 January 1980	146
13	Caging the Beast	151
14	Stonewalling	163

Part VI: Establishing the Truth 1982-95
15	Intimate Ties	186
16	Face to Face	206
17	MI5 Says No	221

Afterword	231
Appendix: Tara Proclamation	237

Acknowledgements

In the sixteen years that I have been collecting information on William McGrath and Kincora, many individuals gave of their time to me at great personal cost, as they relived episodes from their lives that they had thought long since buried. It is impossible to mention them all individually, and, indeed, there are many who wish to remain anonymous. Three people deserve particular acknowledgement for their commitment to trying to come to terms with the real William McGrath and for taking great risks to expose not just his wrongdoings but the activities of MI5, the agency that used and manipulated McGrath for so long. Two are former associates of McGrath – Roy Garland and Clifford Smyth. Without their help and their dogged determination to unearth the truth, this book would not have been possible. The third person is Valerie Shaw, a former missionary in Ian Paisley's Free Presbyterian Church, who showed great courage in 1982 when she spoke out in public on the issue. Others, who include former associates of McGrath, former members of Army Intelligence and police officers, went to great lengths to help me in my research but cannot be publicly identified. To them and to all who valued truth over any political cause, I say thank you.

Thanks also to friends Tony Curry, Mike Nesbitt and Róisín Duffy, who read early drafts of the manuscript and provided critical advice.

In a project such as this, the most vital support comes from home. My wife Fiona and daughter Louise had to tolerate my being a fixture in front of the word processor over the past few months. Without Fiona's unswerving faith in this work, which goes back more than a decade, it might never have been completed. This book is dedicated to her.

Chris Moore
Belfast, January 1996

Author's Note

Since 1980 the name Kincora has been associated in the public mind with homosexual abuse of young men in care, but because of the nature of the media coverage of the story and some wild speculation about the events at Kincora there have been many misconceptions. For example, the word 'prostitution' has been used in relation to the abuses at the hostel in East Belfast but it is quite clear from the evidence of former residents that this allegation is without foundation. In statements to the authorities those abused made allegations only against the three members of staff at Kincora who were subsequently convicted in court. Some made allegations against individuals at other state-run institutions which also resulted in convictions. No one alleged that he was taken to other men for sexual activity or that men came to Kincora to engage in sexual congress with the young men in care there.

Another issue concerns Tara, the group William McGrath established. Initially, it was set up as a ginger group, a talking shop, which was intended to form a cohesive unionist response to the rapidly developing political upheaval of the late 1960s and early 1970s. It must be stressed that Tara was never a proscribed organisation. It provided unionists with a melting pot to take a variety of ideas and develop a strategy to deal with what they viewed as a deteriorating political situation.

Later, McGrath was to use Tara as a means of trying to prepare for a 'doomsday' situation, the day Northern Ireland would face the prospect of British withdrawal and a united Ireland. He used Tara as a pool from which to draw individuals into what he regarded as a paramilitary group, although not paramilitary in the more usual sense of the word – not a group which would conduct a campaign of violence like that of the IRA, UVF or UFF. For instance, although there is some evidence to suggest that a small number of individual members of the group were armed with illegal weapons, Tara itself never engaged in a single 'military operation' during the twenty-five years of conflict in Northern Ireland. McGrath's idea was to prepare a group of men in platoons of twenty, who would not be called upon to fight until 'doomsday' arrived. In the 'doomsday' scenario, law and order would have completely broken down and the Army and RUC would be either disarmed or withdrawn to barracks prior to a total British withdrawal. McGrath's plan was that Tara would step in at this stage and provide leadership for the Protestant people, taking control of the rogue elements of the loyalist paramilitaries and providing support for the legitimate forces of law and order. McGrath was very much against the murderous campaign of tit-for-tat killings conducted by loyalist groups.

Some of the men who attended meetings of Tara were later to become influential figures in unionist circles and it is important to remember that Tara was an entirely legitimate organisation. There is no suggestion that these individuals were at any stage involved in the paramilitary activities described above, nor that they had any knowledge of attempts made by McGrath and by a small number of Tara members to obtain weapons.

Similarly, it must also be stressed that, although

McGrath himself was homosexual, it has never been alleged nor is there any suggestion that any other members of Tara were homosexual.

Again, while there is a suggestion that McGrath may have been working for British intelligence agencies, there is no evidence to suggest that other members of the group were similarly employed or even aware that McGrath may have been an intelligence agent.

Detailed in this book is the extraordinary ability of William McGrath to compartmentalise his life in such a way that even individuals in Tara who were acquainted with one another neither knew nor guessed that McGrath had so many different dimensions to his personality. It was partly the skill with which he managed to do this which enabled him to keep his activities secret for such a long period.

Foreword

The Kincora sex scandal is etched on the collective memory of Northern Ireland. All who have heard the sordid story of the systematic molestation of young victims who were under the care and protection of Northern Ireland's Eastern Health and Social Services Board are left with deep feelings of unease. No other scandal in the province's recent past has prompted so much speculation and rumour. Now we can get as close to the truth as is humanly possible.

Journalistic investigations into the Kincora sex scandal have centred on the personality, character and bizarre motivation of one individual, William McGrath. It was the multi-various, corrupt and sinister activities of McGrath which led to a massive cover-up in Whitehall, a cover-up which to this day withstands attempts to penetrate its wall of secrecy.

This book will expose for the first time the fact that even as McGrath was going to trial for sex offences, a whole litany of criminal activities on behalf of Ulster loyalism was also coming to light. Highly placed security officers charged with the investigation of McGrath's secret world already knew that this middle-aged sex offender had run guns into Northern Ireland. Furthermore, the police knew that McGrath had been instrumental in founding an organisation called Tara. There is evidence to suggest that this organisation may have been controlled and manipulated by British Intelligence for its own ends.

This book will argue that in forming Tara, William

McGrath acted on the directions of his intelligence handlers and that he set in motion events which led directly to the emergence of loyalist paramilitarism or counter-terrorism. He was not alone; others served similar ends. The questions that such evidence raises are devastating. Did British intelligence maintain a shadowy but firm control over loyalist paramilitarism from the early 1970s onwards? Were the innocent lives and future prospects of male adolescents sacrificed to the cynical manipulation of one of the most mysterious and intriguing figures to emerge from the tragedy of Northern Ireland?

It is immediately apparent that the story of William McGrath reaches into the very heart of Northern Ireland's troubles. He was able to build on the fears of grassroots loyalists while promoting a heady doctrine of unionism, evangelicalism and Orange fervour. Given the gravity of the charges contained in this book and the new perspective that such revelations bring to our understanding of the crisis in the North, the reader needs to be assured that the scandal about to unfold is based on careful, tenacious and well documented research, research which has taken the author sixteen years to amass, collate and analyse. In the course of that research the author has interviewed one hundred and three people, many at great length and on numerous occasions. The author has been the recipient of numerous documents from both official and unofficial sources, which have also made a vital contribution to our understanding of William McGrath and the seamy world he inhabited. He found it necessary to broaden the enquiries and the scope of the investigation by making visits to the Republic of Ireland, England and

Scotland and communicating with people now living in France and South Africa.

Because of the nature of these enquiries it has not always been appropriate or possible to publish the names of the author's sources. It will be obvious to the reader when a witness has been given a cover name. All who have contributed to this story are to be commended, particularly those who have allowed their names to go forward.

The real story behind the Kincora cover-up took years to emerge. The author was finally able to dismantle part of the wall of silence and open this sordid affair to the gaze of the public.

Clifford Smyth, loyalist historian,
ex-member Tara and Democratic Unionist Party
Belfast, 1 February 1996

Prologue

Kincora: Trespass and be damned

As I drove along North Road past Van Morrison's Cyprus Avenue the car headlights suddenly fell on the deserted building up ahead at the junction with the Upper Newtownards Road. It was a cold night in January 1982 and I was about to do something of which my bosses at the BBC in Belfast would not have approved. The building on the corner opposite was in complete darkness, as it had been since spring of the previous year, when the police began closing in on the three pederasts who had worked there – all of whom had finally been jailed a few weeks before my journey. It was late and not too many cars or people were travelling what in daylight is a very busy route, so I edged the car through the lights across the Upper Newtownards Road and further along North Road where it disappears down one side of Kincora.

Once past the house I stopped the car, killed the headlights and sat staring straight ahead for a time. Should I or should I not? Even now my commitment to this project was far from definite. My hand reached into my pocket, as if seeking some kind of mystical answer by touching a set of keys which I had been told would secure access to the house; keys provided by someone I had encountered months earlier while researching a background report to follow the trial of Joe Mains, his deputy Raymond Semple and house father William McGrath. It was a fortunate encounter with one of the many individuals who had reason to despise Joe Mains:

> *I am a practising homosexual at the present time and I think that I am the way I am as a result of what Joe Mains did with me when I lived in Kincora. I have a certain amount of resentment towards Joe Mains for what he did with me but I have kept in touch with him because when you are an orphan you have no one other than the people who run the homes you have lived in.*
>
> *Up until I left Kincora both Mains and Semple were interfering with me. I can remember that Mr Mains used to have male friends visit him in Kincora. Sometimes these men would watch TV with the boys or stay in Mr Mains's bedroom with him.*

My heart was beating so loudly as I walked towards the house that I feared it would attract the attention of neighbours. I thought of the suffering of those who had been forced to call this dreadful place 'home' during the previous twenty-four years. The key fitted, the lock yielded and – stomach churning – I was swiftly moving through the side door leading to Joe Mains's living quarters at the rear of the building. The air inside was cold, the atmosphere claustrophobic because of the lack of light and the shadows caused by the street lighting outside. I moved cautiously, looking for the rooms described by my contact for me many times over. Downstairs were the kitchen, the dining room, the television room and the 'office' area, which was dominated by a large desk.

> *Mr McGrath told me to come into the office with him. The office is just beside the kitchen. I walked into the office with Mr McGrath and he did not switch on the light. I was just wearing the bottom of my pyjamas. Mr McGrath then pulled down my pyjama bottoms and rubbed my privates with his hands and he asked me if I was enjoying it. This only happened for a short time and I then pulled my pyjama trousers up and went upstairs. A number of other times Mr McGrath rubbed his hands over my body... I never told Mr Mains or anyone else about what Mr McGrath was doing to me because I was afraid.*
>
> *Mr McGrath and me built up a friendship and used to talk a lot about his religion and the Orange Order.*
>
> *There was once in the kitchen when he [McGrath] came up to me and said something like, 'Did I ever tell you I think you are a nice looking boy?' I asked him what he meant. He said something like 'There is nothing wrong with it, God said it is right to be a homosexual.' He started patting me on the bum. I told him to clear off.*
>
> *On the day I was leaving Kincora Mr McGrath told me that if I had carried on with the massaging a friend of his might have fixed me up with a flat.*

It was in the office area on the ground floor, just where I was told it would be, that I found the little mark on the wall where once the plaque hung for the 'Best Boy of the

Year' award. As one of the former residents remarked to me: 'You know who was most likely to win that trophy, given that Mains was the sole arbiter?'

> *Joe Mains used to take me out in his car, a black Morris Minor. We would drive to Bangor. On one occasion he told me to take the steering and he would work the pedals. I steered the car as it was moving and when Mains's hands were free he opened my zip and wanked me.*

> *Some nights I would be lying in bed in the dormitory when I would hear footsteps on the stairs. I would pretend to be asleep hoping that Mains would not come to my bed. Some nights he would go to the bed of another boy and I watched as he was led off downstairs to Mains's bedroom.*

Up the wide stairs past a grand stained glass window on the first landing to the second landing with bedrooms and bathrooms leading off at various angles.

> *I had sex with McGrath at least three times a week. This always took place in the hostel in either the cloakroom on the ground floor, the sitting-room or in my bedroom. It was nearly always both of us riding each other and sometimes sucking and wanking. At first I did not like it but later I began to enjoy it.*

> *I was transferred to Kincora in the summer of 1973 ... I was about sixteen at the time ... McGrath*

> used to put his penis into my backside and got me to do the same to him . . . I did not know I was doing wrong at the time but I did not like it. I was frightened of McGrath, that is why I did it. I have never told anybody about what happened between Mr McGrath and me. Since the incidents at Kincora I have never done anything like that with another man or boy.

> McGrath boasted about his contacts high up in the Orange Order and loyalist paramilitaries such as the UDA. He boasted of his contacts with top unionist politicians.

As I wandered through the house where so much misery had been visited upon so many, it became increasingly difficult to separate what I knew as fact from what should belong to fiction. At this stage I had no real understanding of the political significance of one of the Kincora three. The house was sparsely furnished. Perhaps some furniture had already been removed – I couldn't tell – but in any event footsteps echoed eerily around this shell of a building and it was impossible to dispel from my thoughts the statements given to the police by some of the young men who had been sexually abused in this place.

> I always had the feeling McGrath was through his influence in the Orange Order . . . and in the group Tara, prodding Northern Ireland as best he could towards the troubles he himself predicted, the blood

on the streets and the holocaust which would accompany the fight for Protestant freedom.

McGrath said the Tara plan was for a 'doomsday' situation.

This visit was to change forever my perspective on the Kincora affair. Up to that point I was simply pursuing a story of administrative failure to investigate reports of sexual abuse of young men in care. Having spent thirteen years covering murder, bloodshed, hardship and grief, I, like so many other reporters, had developed a tough exterior. This was just another assignment, although I was soon to be taken off the newsroom rota and allowed to spend three months full-time on this investigation. But walking around what was basically a shell of a building put flesh on the bones of this story by making my own flesh creep. Standing in the bathroom where I knew that McGrath had carried out a brutal rape, I quietly swore to myself that I would expose the evil of Kincora, that I would not rest until the world knew the truth about William McGrath. It is what that particular rape victim would have wanted more than anything in the world.

Part I
For God and Ulster
1955-67

1
Faith House

William McGrath was born in Belfast during the First World War, on 11 December 1916. His parents lived in Earl Street in the York Road area of the city; his family background was Methodist. McGrath's evangelical work really began when he met his English-born wife Kathleen, who was working in the North Belfast office of the Worldwide Evangelisation Crusade. The McGraths set up home at 40 Ponsonby Avenue in the Antrim Road district in the 1940s, using an upstairs room to run a bible mission. Then for seven years before moving to Wellington Park in 1960, McGrath lived with his wife and three young children in a large house known as Faith House, in the Belfast suburb of Finaghy. It was here that he established the Christian Fellowship and Irish Emancipation Centre. The Belfast street directory for 1952 and 1953 describes McGrath's home as the 'Young People's Christian Fellowship'. It was here that a young man called Roy Garland had an encounter with McGrath in 1955. It was the beginning of a new friendship, the start of a period of Garland's life which would haunt him. It is from Roy Garland that we have the best account of the activities of McGrath at this period.

Roy Garland was born and raised a Protestant on the Shankill Road in Belfast, in a family with a history of Orange associations. His parents, he says, were both 'saved' in 1928; that is to say they had a religious experience, what evangelicals regard as being born again into a Christian lifestyle devoted to God. As a result, Garland's father switched from one Orange lodge to another which accepted only 'saved' men, although he was eventually to leave Orangism completely in the early fifties. It was through a religious mission organised by this same lodge that Garland himself was 'saved' at the age of seven in 1948 after he had pinched some fruit from shops and raided Shankill graveyard for wood for the traditional bonfires on the eve of the Twelfth of July.

Seven years later, Garland was 'saved' again, at a crusade in the King's Hall in Belfast. This time he made a decision not only to 'come back to the Lord' but to dedicate his life to the service of the Lord. A few months after his second religious experience Garland met McGrath. McGrath had been touring mission halls, churches and Orange halls with his message, challenging people to 'Holiness of Life' and dedicated service. On this particular evening, Garland heard McGrath mix religious dogma and political rhetoric. He shocked his audience by warning them of dark days ahead when a great crisis would befall the land and the streets would flow with blood. Central to this message was McGrath's conviction that the IRA had gone 'communist' and was part of a revolutionary movement in Ireland. He made this extraordinary prediction of blood on the streets a full fourteen years before the emergence of the Civil Rights Movement and the subsequent rebirth of the IRA.

McGrath made frequent use of a slide projector to illustrate his arguments. He was fond of showing his home, Faith House in Finaghy, which was owned and maintained by the Christian Fellowship Centre. McGrath told his audiences that Faith House had been bought with cash donated by the Lord's people through 'faith', hence the name Faith House. Other colour slides revealed a decaying church, ivy clinging to the stone walls and moss growing on rafters which had once borne grey slates. The speaker told his mission hall audience that the derelict building on the screen had once been a Protestant church; its dilapidation was evidence, he said, that the Protestant Church in the Republic of Ireland was slowly being destroyed by the policies of a Catholic controlled State.

Using the inbuilt instinct of a good orator, McGrath could vary his talks to suit the audience. Some would be restricted to religious themes; others would put his political analysis in a religious context. Of course there were many audiences which McGrath felt deserved a mixture of the two. Through it all McGrath showed a special interest in the young, taking it upon himself to gather around him those whom he could indoctrinate with his brand of unionism. He saw it as his duty to prepare these young men for a political and spiritual commitment to Christ.

No one knows for certain who indoctrinated McGrath in preparation for his political and evangelical life. In a leaflet he told his followers that all priests and nuns were acting as an army on the direct orders of the Vatican. He believed the Jesuits were actively involved in the infiltration of Protestant churches and culture. His view was that Ireland had once been dominated by an evangelical Celtic church uncontaminated by the teachings of the Roman Catholic Church. This lasted until the 12th Century, when Henry II was given permission by the English Pope Adrian IV to invade Ireland to bring the people there into line with the teachings of the Holy See. McGrath's mission was to bring the island back to that earlier state by eradicating Catholicism and ecumenism.

It was this 'sense of history' which motivated McGrath and gave him an unusual perspective for a Protestant, a sense of Irishness. McGrath said the denial of Irishness was a relatively recent development of unionist politicians, dating since partition, and McGrath was unhappy with partition. Pamphlets were issued from Faith House with prayers that Ireland would one day be set free. Under the heading, 'Freedom: What is it?' McGrath had this to say: 'The Irish Emancipation Crusade and Christian Fellowship Centre was founded in the year 1941 by a group of Irishmen for the purpose of setting their country free from those things which prevent her reaching the full stature of her nationhood.'

This pamphlet was designed to reach nationalists and was distributed in Dublin at big sporting events. A page was headed, 'God Save Ireland,' and quoted the words of a song attributed to T. D. Sullivan: 'God Save Ireland said the heroes/God Save Ireland, said they all.' Two shamrocks flanked another heading, written by McGrath himself:

> To know Ireland is to love her,
> To love Ireland is to serve her,
> To serve Ireland is to lead her back to God,
> *Nothing Else Matters!*

In this pamphlet McGrath did not openly ask his readers to help to rid Ireland of Catholicism. Later, when he moved to Wellington Park, one of his works, called 'The Twin Evils of our Time – Romanism – Communism', articulated more bluntly his opposition to Catholicism.

> Seemingly striving in opposite directions, these twin evils are under the control of Satan. Their aim is the destruction of the people of God and the Testimony of our Lord Jesus Christ. For the Christian there can be no choice between Romanism and Communism. Both are evil. The darkest crimes of Communism have been equalled a thousand times by the so-called Roman Catholic 'Church'. We cannot ally ourselves with one against the other. We dare not surrender to one because of fear of the other!

Roy Garland had mixed feelings as he left the mission hall that first night. Although he was impressed by the 'Challenge of Ireland' scenario presented by McGrath, he instinctively felt there was something not altogether wholesome about the man. McGrath took a special interest in the teenage Garland, going out of his way to invite him to visit his headquarters. Within a few weeks Garland found himself making his way towards Finaghy on a dark November night. He recalls going along Orpen Park and finding a notice board at the end of a lane with the words Faith House in large letters. He was deeply impressed by this massive family mansion, apparently built by Huguenots. Life at Faith House, McGrath's 'fellowship', was based on what its originator described as an ancient Celtic tradition, a kind of monastic structure. McGrath himself was married with children but he expected those who were part of the community (mostly young men) to be unmarried and to devote themselves entirely to the Lord. Lodgers contributed part of their income towards their upkeep and the maintenance of the house. According to the gospel of William McGrath, this pooling of their wages was to fund the salvation of Ireland, north and south. It was here, right under the nose of his wife and children, that McGrath set out to help his young house guests to resolve their sexual problems, talking individually to them about 'emotional blocks' which he said could be released if they had close, but not sexual, relationships with people of their own sex.

Kathleen McGrath was aware of the good work her husband William did with young men, and occasionally young women. Young and old were sent to him by various people for help; for example problem children from Dr Barnardo's homes would be sent to McGrath. Garland says it is important to understand that McGrath's work with young people was not exclusively concerned with sexual matters and that there was definitely a positive side to it:

I saw young men who came into contact with McGrath begin to take an interest in themselves. Some – maybe most – of the older men who had been in contact with McGrath in the 1940s had been motivated to develop their ability and were successful in the careers they followed, even achieving academic qualifications and high political office. So some said McGrath had given them a sense of worth and dignity. This side of McGrath must be understood and set alongside the corruption which he became increasingly involved in. His activities at Kincora seem so out of keeping with the man, the family man, as to be unrecognisable. Even for me it is hard to reconcile what happened in Kincora with the happy and loving family man he was most of the time.

At this very first meeting in Faith House, Garland had a confusing experience. During the discussion that was taking place, McGrath touched Garland's leg and then asked the fifteen-year-old what it meant to him. Shocked, the young Garland said it meant nothing. When it happened again, the youngster told him it meant nothing. What happened next is enlightening, although Garland did not realise it at the time. This is how he described it in *The Irish Times*, in April 1982:

> I assumed this was some kind of test, and he went on to talk about the very high standards which were required of young people in relation to sex. Even holding a girl's hand was to be discouraged as it

could lead to sexual arousal in the girl and the dissipation of emotional energy which should be devoted to God. He asked me to return in a month or so and after some initial doubt I returned. He continued to talk about politics and sex but always in the context of Christian service. While he condemned homosexual relationships he told me that a balanced individual must have a close relationship with a member of his own sex. He said that David and Jonathan, Jesus and John, the beloved disciple, had close friendships which had a physical side to them. He quoted the verse of a hymn: 'Touched by a loving hand, wakened by kindness/chords that were broken will vibrate once more.' I thought about this and then accused him of being a homosexual, though I did not really know what this meant. At this point he introduced me to his wife and family and this calmed my fears.

However, the message seemed clear enough. Men could, even in biblical times, love one another in a physical way. It was an argument McGrath would use again and again in the future. In the years ahead many young men would learn that the lines from the hymn had a literal meaning for McGrath as he attempted to satisfy his pederasty: 'Touched by a loving hand, wakened by kindness . . . ' As many Kincora boys were to tell the police years later, they would frequently be woken in the morning by McGrath's hands under the bedclothes touching their private parts.

As time went on, McGrath's extremism made Garland uneasy. In spite of some reservations, Garland also acknowledged the kindness of the McGrath family; he occasionally stayed for meals cooked by Kathleen. It was McGrath who, in the late 1950s, steered Garland away from a career in the army to follow his desire to become a missionary. He directed him to a bible college near Windsor, where he began his studies in September 1960.

According to a senior police source McGrath had already done his bit to combat the threat of communism by opening up a secret channel of supply to Christian contacts in Iron Curtain countries. His illicit trade was in bibles and religious literature. It was this clandestine business enterprise that was ultimately to provide him with protection from prosecution for his activities as a homosexual and pederast for an extended period. In 1958 McGrath travelled to Dublin to meet someone with connections behind the Iron Curtain, possibly a KGB agent, as the RUC was to discover during its investigations in 1980-3. As McGrath had already been traced by the British Secret Service, MI6, his movements were by now being closely monitored. His visit to Dublin was observed in the belief that McGrath might lead the British secret service to a KGB agent. Certainly it was a crucial development: as McGrath himself was later to tell some of his followers it was after this meeting that MI6 approached him, seeking his help. They wanted to make use of his communications network to pass messages back and forth behind the Iron Curtain. The McGrath bibles would provide perfect cover for such underground activity at a time when the Cold War was at its zenith.

From this point onwards, my source said, McGrath was

hooked into the British establishment underworld network and would eventually become an agent for the state. Everything he did from this point on was known to his contacts in MI6, and, later on, MI5, when in the early 1970s they took over control of operations in Northern Ireland. The British encouraged McGrath to intensify his political activities to help create the climate for an exchange of information. They would supply McGrath with intelligence to pass on to his audiences in public or to his followers in private. One obvious outlet from the 1960s on was Ian Paisley's *Protestant Telegraph*. At one time, for instance, historian and political activist Clifford Smyth was contributing articles, as was the South Antrim MP, Sir Knox Cunningham. While McGrath was massaging the facts he was feeding to his attentive unionist and Protestant gatherings, he would also be helping the British intelligence network to keep its finger on the pulse of the Protestant-unionist community.

In the mid-1960s, Garland and other members of the Christian Fellowship began accompanying McGrath on his tours to watch him speak at engagements in mission halls, Orange halls and at meetings of Young Unionists. In 1961, while Garland was in college in England, McGrath travelled over for a campaign in mission halls and churches in England. Garland was present at a meeting he addressed in own college and at another in a London bible college. Once McGrath asked Garland to meet him at the Foreign Missions Club in London but this turned out to be an extremely unsatisfactory meeting as McGrath left Garland to attend to some business which he felt he could not disclose or discuss with his young protégé. He did tell Garland that he had visited the offices of the *Daily Mail* regarding an article on Hungary, a country which McGrath felt bore comparison with Ireland. He also described giving a lecture in an Anglican church in which the vicar, according to McGrath, was a communist. McGrath was to become a frequent visitor to London, telling his followers that these meetings were crucial to the wellbeing of Northern Ireland.

When Garland returned to Northern Ireland after his studies in England, McGrath encouraged him to become more deeply involved in unionist politics, which led, much later, to his turning away from his socialist leanings to more right-wing politics. At one point Garland had an unusual experience, similar to experiences which others were later to have. Anonymous letters began to arrive for Garland, suggesting that he was being groomed for political leadership. The letters claimed to come from influential individuals associated with McGrath, who were interested in the welfare of the British Isles in general and Northern Ireland in particular. When Garland challenged McGrath, McGrath claimed to know who had written the letters but would not give any names and denied that he had any involvement.

This was taking place against a backdrop of growing political instablility. All the while McGrath was gathering into his religious-political group young men he singled out as having political potential, men who in later years became familiar names in unionism. In the next decade McGrath could, at various times, count among his audience people like Clifford Smyth, prominent loyalist historian and ex-DUP member, Fraser Agnew, Jeremy Burchill, Frank Millar Junior, Reg Empey, John Laird – all prominent in unionist circles at various times; James Heyburn, Paisley's general secretary for many years (whose involvement with McGrath ceased a short time after Tara was founded), and David Browne, deputy editor of Paisley's *Protestant Telegraph*. There were also Ian Dawson, Alan Gingles and Charles Simpson, members of the group called Tara, who went to Africa and fought with the Rhodesian security forces. Like Garland, they were encouraged to believe they were being specially groomed as future leaders of the Protestant-unionist community. This furthered McGrath's reputation as a man who did not lead from the front, but who could provide leadership from behind the scenes. And, of course, by the mid-1960s, McGrath had access to some of the main players in unionism, like James Molyneaux, Ian Paisley and John Bryans, head of the Orange Order. It was in the mid-1960s that a young man called Dave (his name has been changed for security reasons) read a religious tract called 'The Shame of Belfast' which was handed to him in a Belfast street and was attracted to visit the Christian Fellowship Centre in Wellington Park. He was to find that there was more to McGrath than evangelical religion – and more again than paramilitary politics.

The mission halls and Orange halls echoed to the message of impending political conflict as McGrath prepared Protestants for the fight to save Ulster from a variety of enemies. As the IRA's unsuccessful border campaign of 1956–62 ground to an end, McGrath was again telling anyone who would listen that blood would be flowing in the streets of Belfast, urging them to prepare for the onslaught against their faith and freedom by, among other things, the sinister forces in the Catholic Church. When he addressed religious bodies in church halls, at evangelical gatherings or at Unionist Party meetings, his message was to stress the need for prayers and to be prepared for conflict. Yet at other meetings he would happily speak in the vein of one of his 1962 leaflets calling for preparations for action to deal with the coming crisis. His leaflet said: '... we will be labelled as bigots and our actions described as undemocratic. When our fathers ran the guns into Bangor and Larne, their action was undemocratic, illegal and unconstitutional, but God blessed their efforts and gave us the victory. The spirit of our fathers must live again in us.'

2
CELL BECOMES TARA

By 1965, Garland was invited to join a discussion organisation which, according to him, had the name 'Cell'. It was a private ginger group of Orangemen under the chairmanship of a Church of Ireland clergyman, the Reverend S. E. Long, whose name, some reports say, was the real source of the name of the group: the acronym S. E. L. Clifford Smyth, who is among the pivotal sources for much of McGrath's career, remembers his first encounter with this group at McGrath's house in Wellington Park in 1966. (Faith House had been sold by the Christian Fellowship and the house in Wellington Park bought from them by McGrath for his own use.) By this time Smyth had begun to build a reputation as a skilled debater. He had been rapidly promoted within the Orange order and was now one of his lodge's delegates to Number Two Orange District. What Smyth himself describes as 'a vigorous Protestant speech from the body of the hall' on the occasion of his first meeting as a delegate brought him to the attention of District Secretary Lindsay Smyth (no relation). It was Lindsay who told Clifford about an Orange ginger group which had been established to discuss issues affecting the order.

Lindsay told Clifford, who had recently joined the Young Unionists, that he spoke like a British Israelite, and Clifford recalled a bizarre meeting a few days earlier when a stranger approached him as he studied books in the Evangelical Bookshop in College Square East. As he stood by a rack of books published by the Protestant Truth Society, Clifford felt uneasy because of the intensity of the gaze of the young stranger and when he moved in to begin a conversation, Clifford made his excuses and left in a hurry, pausing only to draw breath at the window of the Presbyterian Bookshop in Howard Street. But the young stranger was swiftly at his shoulder, trying to persuade Clifford that the British people were descended from the lost tribes of Israel. This was an argument Clifford could not accept and eventually he made his escape. Now he was being told that he talked like a British Israelite.

Eventually Lindsay persuaded Clifford to turn up for the next meeting of the Orange ginger group, at 15 Wellington Park. It was to be an eventful meeting.

Clifford Smyth has written about this meeting in some detail in an as yet unpublished work about his life in politics in Northern Ireland and the influence of the enigmatic William McGrath. With his permission I quote the following extracts, starting with his arrival for his first meeting of 'Cell' at McGrath's house:

> Fifteen Wellington Park was an imposing terrace house, just off the Malone Road, near Queen's University. I arrived punctually for the meeting of this Orange ginger group, dressed in my Sunday best. A middle-aged man of about five foot eight in height and medium build greeted me with a firm handshake. 'We are up the stairs,' he beckoned. 'There are a few still to come.' I was led up a flight of stairs to one of the largest living rooms I had

ever entered. There was a deep red Wilton carpet on the floor and the room was neatly but not ostentatiously furnished. The suite of armchairs and the sofa all had loose covers, giving the room a certain utilitarian air. There were already about ten others in the room; most were older, even much older than I was. The meeting soon got under way. The Reverend S. E. Long, a Church of Ireland cleric, acted as a kind of chairman and there speedily followed a round of introductions. I did not immediately place all the others. Lindsay Smyth was there, as was Major Hyndes, the District Master of Number Two. The others were unknown to me. The Reverend S. E. Long explained why the meeting had been convened. I listened intently.

Clifford Smyth heard a debate about the condition of the Orange institution which he says 'lit up' the evening and clearly demonstrated divisions among those present. It quickly became apparent that the Reverend Long and some of the other older brethren present saw matters very differently, and Clifford was compelled to ask himself if he was too right-wing, an extremist. There was a familiarity about the debate; had his opinions not met with similar resistance during wine and cheese soirées of the Young Unionists? He finally felt the need to reveal his colours and, exasperated by what he saw as the complacent stance of his elders, Clifford said, 'You see, I am a committed Christian.' He intended this statement to beg the question whether Anglicans were less committed, too close to popery. This is how he describes what happened next:

I noticed that the gentleman who had ushered me into the house was agreeing with me. The light in the lounge caught the lens of his glasses and there was a glister of hair cream from the strands that crossed his thinning scalp. When he spoke there was an intensity and passion in his voice which belied his demeanour. Lindsay turned to me and grinned. Clearly he was enjoying the debate, but was unwilling to declare in favour either of the Reverend Ernie Long's moderation or those of us who held that the Church of Rome was not Christian but a gross deception which had to be resisted. There could be no conclusion to such an evening, so other than agreeing that this new group should adopt the acronym 'SEL', derived from the initials of our chairman, not much else was decided.

But there *was* one other significant event that evening, for as Clifford left the house he was taken to one side by Lindsay and introduced to 'our host'.

> ... he stood beside the chair he had occupied all evening, dressed in a bottle-green knitted woollen cardigan with highly polished brown shoes and pressed flannels. Lindsay Smyth turned and said, 'Clifford, this is the brother I told you about before, who knows so much about what is going on beneath the surface; truly remarkable information.' Lindsay paused. 'Meet William McGrath.' McGrath nodded his head and he smiled, a tight little knowing smile.

In the coming months, Clifford Smyth's curiosity about McGrath grew as he was drawn deeper into the workings of the older man's ginger group. The attitude of the group's chairman, the Reverend S. E. Long, clearly perplexed McGrath. It was obvious that the clergyman regarded Catholics as no less Christians than Presbyterian, a viewpoint that unsettled McGrath.

The impetus to set up his own Orange ginger group in the mid-1960s almost certainly came from the promptings of McGrath's contacts in British intelligence and a major political development that year gave him the perfect cover. The unionist community was shaken to its foundations by the activities of the Northern Ireland Prime Minister Captain Terence O'Neill, who for a long time had been regarded by McGrath as an able politician trying to save Ulster. But now, like so many others, McGrath began to feel betrayed by O'Neill, who accepted office in 1963 on a reformist ticket, undertaking firstly to strengthen cross-border economic links and secondly to try to find an accommodation with the political ambitions of the increasingly well educated Catholic population. However, O'Neill overstepped the mark in January 1965 when he entertained the Republic's Taoiseach Sean Lemass at Stormont, the symbol of Protestant power.

Guided by his intelligence handlers, McGrath eventually put his talking shop to work in the campaign to unseat O'Neill, a campaign spearheaded by Ian Paisley, who organised a number of protests against the new developments. By now McGrath had begun to put himself about in the loyalist community, active in a range of organisations, both religious and political. His own 'Cell' group met to discuss the impending doom; he continued his talks at Orange halls and at a sprinkling of meetings of unionists. By now he could number among his friends and acquaintances many senior unionist politicians, including a couple in the Stormont cabinet – or so he told some of his followers at the weekly meetings. (It was apparently his involvement with the Unionist Association in the Shore Road area in 1949 which brought him into contact with Paisley, who had moved into the area to live while he studied at a bible college. This was the beginning of what McGrath was later to regard as a long friendship between the two men and their families.)

The unionist population began to fracture over whether or not to support O'Neill's reforms and McGrath intensified his warnings that the gun would soon be required to defend the faith against the three 'isms', Romanism, republicanism and communism (soon a fourth 'ism', liberalism, was added). Among his audiences was a small group of Shankill Road men who, along with others in rural areas, were motivated by O'Neill's meeting with Lemass to consider forming an armed gang which would revive the name of Carson's UVF. This force had valiantly fought and died as the 36th (Ulster) Division of the British Army during the Battle of the Somme in the First World War. Garland told me that McGrath seemed to be aware of this development and viewed it in a positive light, although the socialism of the UVF later made it suspect in his eyes.

As the campaign against O'Neill continued in 1966, there came the first tangible evidence of the formation of the UVF. McGrath now believed that the armed group was organised at a very high level. A few days after the

UVF delivered a statement announcing 'war on the IRA' [on 21 May] John Scullion, a Catholic, was fatally wounded by UVF members. The next killing came during the marching season and followed the annual Orange Whiterock parade from the Shankill. The parade was a propaganda opportunity for McGrath: on this occasion the leaflet issued by the Christian Fellowship and Irish Emancipation Centre was entitled, 'The National Crisis of Faith,' which, it said, would 'eventually break into armed conflict between those who fight the battles of the Lord against the might and those who know nothing of the glorious liberty of the children of God.' McGrath's followers recall that this leaflet was inspired by those in London who had an interest in McGrath and his political development. That very night, barman Peter Ward and three workmates from the International Hotel were drinking in the Malvern Arms on the Shankill Road. As they left the pub in the early hours they were attacked by a UVF gang. Eighteen-year-old Ward was shot dead and two of his companions wounded, purely on sectarian grounds. It was 26 June 1966. Perhaps the best known UVF leader of all, Gusty Spence, was one of the group that was also drinking in the Malvern Arms and that decided to kill the four young Catholics. Also sitting in the bar that night was a small group of off-duty policemen and it was no surprise that within hours they had helped the investigating officers to identify those likely to have been involved. The arrest of Spence and others contributed to a further raising of the political temperature and prompted severe clashes between Prime Minister O'Neill and Paisley.

Paisley had been busy during the year, leading the

'O'Neill must go' campaign and taking part in street demonstrations not only against the Prime Minister, but also against what he viewed as the ecumenical and liberal attitudes of the Presbyterian Church. On 6 June, for example, he organised a parade through Cromac Square to Fisherwick Place, where he intended to picket the Presbyterian General Assembly. McGrath was not involved in this demonstration because he viewed as misguided Paisley's attempts to drive a wedge between the churches and the Unionist Party. He did, however, become involved in the Paisley-inspired Ulster Constitution Defence Committee (UCDC) which in turn had close links with a paramilitary grouping, the Ulster Protestant Volunteers (UPV). Members of these groups mounted counter-demonstrations to Republican Easter parades marking the fiftieth anniversary of the Easter Rising. The banners McGrath prepared for Paisley's demonstration carried slogans such as, 'For God and Ireland' and 'By Right of Calvary, Ireland belongs to Christ', painted against green, white and orange backgrounds. Garland regarded them as inappropriate but recalled that many loyalists seemed to be moved emotionally by them.

The UCDC attracted hardline members from the loyalist community. At a meeting to recruit members for the UPV in Lisburn Orange Hall on 10 May 1966 Paisley pledged that divisions of the movement would be established in every parliamentary constituency. At this meeting Paisley was presented with a 1912 UVF cap badge by the chairman of the movement, William Belshaw, a close political and evangelical associate of McGrath, who proclaimed that the new Volunteers would be guided by the same motto: 'For God and Ulster'. By the time the UVF murdered Ward, Paisley had already been accused of publicly stating he enjoyed the support of members of the UVF, an allegation which he denied. Within hours of the murder, Terence O'Neill moved to proscribe the organisation which, the Prime Minister said, had misappropriated the name 'UVF'. One of Spence's co-accused, Hugh McClean, is alleged to have replied to police when charged: 'I am terribly sorry I ever heard tell of that man Paisley or decided to follow him. I am definitely ashamed of myself to be in such a position.' Paisley's response to this was one of outright condemnation: 'This is to try to tie me up with this atrocious murder. I do not know Mr McClean. He is not a Free Presbyterian ... Mr McClean never was a member of the UCDC, never was a member of the UPV divisions and he has never been associated with me at all.'

With Spence and his co-accused locked up in the remand wing of Crumlin Road Jail in Belfast, McGrath was harnessing public support for the UVF leader in his pending trial. But as Garland recalls, there was another angle to this. In September 1966 McGrath asked Garland to join him on a visit to see Paisley at his church. Once there, McGrath informed Paisley that two clergymen in the Orange Order had linked him [Paisley] to the UVF. According to Garland, Paisley said he would immediately seek legal advice because he regarded the suggestion as defamatory. McGrath then produced a number of anonymous sheets dissociating Paisley from the UVF and also aimed at saving Spence from the death sentence and at presenting the UVF murder victims as communists. In one leaflet

McGrath stated that the UVF had been reconstituted as a paramilitary force at the behest of a member or members of the ruling party of government, the Unionists. He went so far as to say that some members of the Unionist Party had provided weapons for the UVF, but he stopped short of naming names. McGrath implied that he knew which unionists had been behind the formation of this 'private army' and why the UVF had been encouraged to set themselves up as the saviours of Ulster. No evidence has ever been produced to substantiate this. Garland is certain that during this time McGrath supported the actions of the UVF. 'I imagine,' he said, 'that McGrath wanted to save Paisley because he was very important in getting McGrath's political analysis across.'

McGrath's document certainly had an impact. On the opening day of Spence's trial on 3 October 1966, the Lord Chief Justice, Lord MacDermott, addressed the jury which had just been sworn in: 'It has come to my notice that certain communications, through the post or otherwise, have been sent to various members of the community regarding this case and other cases that still have to be tried at the Commission. You should disregard all communications of that kind, they may be anonymous or not, but disregard them completely.' He instructed the jurors to decide on the evidence of the case, and nothing else.

At the time of the Spence trial, McGrath gave Clifford Smyth a copy of a document entitled, 'The Truth About the UVF and the Ward and Scullion Murders.' It was typed, he says, on a single sheet of white quarto paper. Smyth has this document in his possession to this day. It linked as communist the names of the two young Catholics who had become the first victims of loyalist sectarian violence and then it claimed: 'Some years ago there was formed in Belfast an organisation [previously unheard of] known as "Ulster Protestant Action". This was a militant but unarmed movement dedicated to stemming the ever-increasing threat of Roman Catholic domination in the Six Counties.' As Smyth was quick to spot, the term 'Six Counties' is used by nationalists, never by loyalists, and he thought that this was perhaps an attempt to throw the authorities off the scent of the author. The document continued:

> At the time there was much IRA activity in the country and the Official Unionist Party saw the U.P.A. as a possible basis for underground movement to counter IRA activity. Eventually the U.P.A. was infiltrated by Official Unionist Party agents who in a short time took over complete control. The Ulster Volunteer Force was then formed as an armed underground movement by those who had gained control of the U.P.A. During the Kelfedder [*sic*] election in West Belfast arms were issued freely by the Party to members of the Ulster Volunteer Force.

The purpose of this document was twofold. Firstly, it was designed to smear the Official Unionist Party by making false allegations in regard to their involvement in paramilitary activities and arming members of a paramilitary organisation. Secondly, McGrath also clearly intends to deter his readers from concluding that this sinister gathering of armed men who had stolen the good name of the heroes of the Battle of the Somme had been heavily influenced by Paisley's political rhetoric. Notice also the misspelling of Jim Kilfedder's name, perhaps another attempt to hide the origins of the document. The concluding paragraphs referred directly to the two young murder victims:

> Ward was an enemy agent who was working in co-operation with Rose, the anti-Ulster MP at Westminster. The International Hotel, Donegall Square, Belfast, is a favourite meeting place for Enemy Agents and in many ways is their HQ. Ward was employed here. Scullion while still remaining a nominal RC was an active Communist engaged in bringing Communist Arms into the Six Counties and Éire. Mr Diamond, Republican Labour MP for Falls, suggested in the Commons that Scullion was murdered not by extreme Protestants but by 'people of another political character.' What does Diamond know of Communist gun-running?

Having read this, Smyth asked McGrath directly if he had written it. McGrath nodded and murmured, 'It had to be done.' As Smyth has written: 'McGrath had lifted the veil on one more compartment of his life. Within five years, I would look back on all these events in 1966 as the prologue to Ulster's apparently endless civil strife.'

When, in 1990, I spoke to Gusty Spence about McGrath, he told me there had been an approach to him in 1965 by two people, one a unionist politician, informing him there was to be a new UVF. He was clear that the new UVF was not established because of any threat from the IRA. In Spence's opinion it was organised as part of the right-wing unionist opposition to the liberal thinking of Prime Minister O'Neill, perhaps to be used as some kind of lever to put pressure on O'Neill and those within unionist circles who approved of his actions. As far as I am aware, Gusty Spence has not made public the name of the unionist who approached him in the first instance. But he does believe he was used as a pawn in a political game and he recalls vividly the strange line of questioning from the detectives who arrested him. 'The one question they kept asking me was about a plot for a coup d'état,' Spence recalled. 'This was the year of marching men, of rebellion from within the ruling Unionist Party by hardliners who objected to the policies of O'Neill. The only coup that year was the internal plot within the Unionist Party to get rid of O'Neill.'

Meanwhile, as the political temperature rose dramatically during 1966, McGrath found himself at odds with the chairman of 'Cell', the clergyman who clearly was not adopting a hard enough line. McGrath contrived to have the clergyman removed from office in November – a month after the conclusion of the Spence trial – and seized tighter control of the organisation in order to engineer the adoption of a harder line. He changed its name to Tara and took over as chairman.

McGrath himself chose the name Tara, which was an early indication of his desire to maintain an Irish identity: Tara is the hill in county Meath where the high kings of ancient Ireland were crowned. McGrath believed all Irish, Scottish, Welsh and English to be among the tribes of Israel. Catholics, therefore, were also Israelites, but deceived by their priests and living in spiritual darkness. McGrath was a British Israelite and held meetings of this organisation in his home. Among those who attended at one time or another were Orange leader John Bryans and Unionist MP the Reverend Robert Bradford. McGrath and the British Israelites believed that the coronation stone in Westminster Abbey had at one time been located at Tara and that it had originally been Jacob's pillow.

One of the young men attracted to the British Israelite meetings at McGrath's home in Wellington Park was Dave. Clifford Smyth made the discovery at his second or third meeting in McGrath's house, not of the British Israelites but of 'Cell', that the young man who ushered him into the house was the same young man who had pursued him in the Christian bookshop. It was here that Clifford was formally introduced to Dave.

Tara's slogan said it all: 'We hold Ulster that Ireland might be saved and Britain reborn.' Tara was to be the vehicle by which the undercover elements of the British establishment would lift McGrath's star into the political ascendancy.

Meanwhile McGrath's influence within Belfast Orangism was on the increase. As chaplain of the prestigious Fernhill Orange Lodge he had access to Belfast's Number 2 District Orange Lodge, where he gained the ear of some of the city's leading Orangemen. Because of his work with the Lowe Memorial Presbyterian Church in the 1940s, he already knew the Reverend Martin Smyth who had been a clergyman at this church in the Finaghy area and of course he was well known to John Bryans, his former bible study teacher. At Clifton Street Orange Hall he would set out the stall for a 'doomsday' scenario. By 'doomsday' he meant the point at which the union between Northern Ireland and Britain would be on the verge of disintegration. This, he said, would occur as a result of an invasion of Northern Ireland by the army of the Irish Republic, followed by a demand for the deployment of an international peace-keeping force. Tara would have in place a plan for a provisional government and a paramilitary force to support the existing security forces.

It was at these Orange meetings that McGrath began to reveal the extent of the knowledge fed to him by unidentified 'government' intelligence sources. It was at these meetings that he would tell those who challenged his views that they should never 'question the word of an intelligence officer'.

Part II
Ulster at the Crossroads 1968–71

3
What Kind of Ulster?

When I left Ballymoney in County Antrim with my family in 1963 to set up home in Scotland, I went with a tear in my eye and absolutely no understanding of the religious and political strains on those I left behind. By the time our family moved back in 1968 it was obvious that everything had changed – McGrath could be forgiven for gloating that his predictions of civil disorder were bearing a bitter fruit. It was a turbulent political year, a year which began badly and got worse. Prime Minister O'Neill pressed ahead with his plans for reforms and with his newly established relationship with the Irish Republic. He went south to Dublin on 8 January to continue his dialogue with the government there on a range of issues described as 'non-contentious', issues such as cultural exchanges and foot-and-mouth disease.

Signs of strain were evident during the summer months as housing became the focal point of nationalist objections to the system of government which, they argued, favoured the Protestant-unionist community. The dam burst in October. A Civil Rights Association protest march over discrimination in housing went ahead in Derry on the fifth of the month, in spite of a ban placed on it two days earlier by Stormont Home Affairs Minister, William Craig. His justification was that there was likely to be disorder because the Apprentice Boys were scheduled to parade that same day. Things were never to be the same again. The parade clashed with police trying to enforce the banning order. The resulting disturbances marked the beginning of twenty-five years of conflict, murder and mayhem. Even though a month later, on 22 November, the Northern Ireland government fulfilled its promise of producing a five-point reform programme, it appeared it was too little, too late. The type of disorder witnessed in Derry began to spread to other centres and by December, O'Neill felt compelled to try to calm things down by appearing on television with a 'save the nation' address. By this time he faced rebellion from within the ranks of his own party and had sacked one member of his cabinet, William Craig, who warned:

> It has been by the grace of God that civil war has not already been created in Northern Ireland. The temperature is at a boiling point that I have never known in my lifetime. One of these days one of these marches is going to get a massive reaction from the population. Ordinary decent people have been at boiling point for some time. It is not just Mr Paisley.

This comment came a week before O'Neill's television address, as violence spread to towns all over Northern Ireland with the revolt of nationalists against unionist discrimination and abuse of power and an ever-increasing number of unionist-loyalist counter-demonstrations orchestrated by individuals like Paisley.

O'Neill's television and radio broadcast on 9 December 1968 had an air of desperation, of a final appeal for reason. It was an attempt to bypass his cabinet critics and seek support directly from the public. It became known as the 'crossroads' address.

> Ulster stands at the crossroads. I believe you know me well enough by now to appreciate that I am not a man given to extravagant language. But I must say to you this evening that our conduct over the coming days and weeks will decide our future... These issues are far too serious to be determined behind closed doors or left to noisy minorities. The time has come for the people as a whole to speak in a clear voice. For more than five years now I have tried to heal some of the deep divisions in our community. I did so because I could not see how an Ulster divided against itself could hope to stand. I made it clear that a Northern Ireland based upon the interests of any one section rather than upon the interests of all could have no long-term future. Throughout the community many people have responded warmly to my words. But if Ulster is to become the happy and united place it could be,

> there must be the will throughout our Province and particularly in Parliament, to translate these words into deeds ... There are, I know, today some so-called Loyalists who talk of independence from Britain, who seem to want a kind of Protestant Sinn Féin ... Unionism armed with justice will be a stronger Unionism armed merely with strength ... What kind of Ulster do you want? A happy and respected Province in good standing with the rest of the United Kingdom? Or a place continually torn apart by riots and demonstrations and regarded by the rest of Britain as a political outcast?

More than 150,000 citizens sent letters of support to O'Neill and three days after his speech he got the backing of Unionist MPs at Stormont, although, significantly, four abstained.

One thing is certain: William McGrath did not write any of the 150,000 letters of support. He was actively involved in briefing his followers about the doom 'Ulster' faced if O'Neill's policies of appeasement of the Catholic minority were allowed to continue and develop.

By the time of O'Neill's television address, Dave had grown accustomed to McGrath's predictions and, like so many others over the years, he noted his mentor's strange ability to forecast political developments. After the initial British Israelite meeting, Dave had decided to join the Orange Order and this, by chance, led to a second encounter with McGrath. He arranged to meet John Bryans. As they were leaving Clifton Street Orange Hall they bumped into

McGrath. Bryans stopped McGrath and told him about Dave's interest in joining the Order. At the time McGrath was chaplain to Fernhill Lodge, reportedly the largest lodge in the country. A few weeks later Dave received a letter from Fernhill inviting him to join, although, as it turned out, it was a short-lived membership and a short-lived association with McGrath.

In 1968 Dave found himself at the centre of a lodge row over whether or not they should be represented at a street demonstration during a visit to Northern Ireland by the Bishop of Ripon, Dr John Moorman, a controversial ecumenist who was the Church of England's observer to the Vatican Council and leader of an Anglican group involved with talks with Catholic theologians in Italy about unity. Dave, McGrath and two others were on the verge of setting up a new lodge, the Cross of St Patrick, when the controversy began within Fernhill Lodge about the Bishop's proposed visit. McGrath was campaigning inside the lodge for a big protest outside St Anne's Cathedral to coincide with one being planned by Paisley and sought a meeting with Dave to discuss two points. They drove from Belfast to Bangor on the County Down coast and McGrath first attempted to persuade Dave to use his influence on other lodge members to secure their support for his planned protest. Dave listened but expressed no opinion and, realising he was not making progress in this area, McGrath then went on to the second point, which in a nutshell concerned his designs on Dave. Dave told me he was shocked by McGrath's talk of man loving his fellow man, even in a physical sense. He brought the car to a halt and told McGrath bluntly that as far as he was concerned physical love should be strictly confined to man and woman. The journey home was in silence, save for the occasional remark from McGrath to the effect that he hoped he had not offended his friend. Once Dave dropped McGrath off, he drove immediately to a friend's house to report the bizarre happening, only to be stunned by his friend's admission that he already knew about McGrath's homosexuality. Unwilling to let the matter drop, Dave and another friend then approached a leading Orange Order official but their conversation with him was very brief. Dave remembered finding it difficult to contain his anger on being asked if he was married. His lasting impression of the meeting was of being told to go home and forget about it.

This was a difficult time for Dave because of the proposed establishment of a new lodge. In spite of his problems with McGrath he went ahead for the sake of the others involved, although he continued to spread the word privately about McGrath's sexuality. One evening before a lodge meeting McGrath took Dave to one side and threatened to sue him if he did not stop spreading stories about him. That brief conversation was virtually the only one they had since the trip to Bangor. On 10 June 1968, McGrath left the Cross of St Patrick LOL 688 to join St Mary's Fellowship Temperance LOL 1303, the lodge he would soon take over and lead to its ultimate destruction. With McGrath out of the way, Dave continued to take every opportunity to speak out about him. He no longer attended the prayer meetings in McGrath's home but, like Garland, he still saw most of his friends, who had become involved in the various organisations now under McGrath's influence. He began to receive threatening letters because he was speaking out against McGrath and during a later visit to Scotland when he was a member of Vanguard a woman warned him not to say a word about the Tara leader. This did not deter him from informing a group of elderly people who had been approached by McGrath for money to buy arms. He passed on to other leading unionist politicians his knowledge of McGrath's sexual orientation. The people he spoke to included family friend Jim Molyneaux, later leader of the Unionist Party, who called frequently at Dave's house for tea. Dave was disappointed by the reaction he got, although it is not clear what he expected Molyneux to do about it, or, indeed, what Molyneaux could have done about it. Garland remembers Molyneaux calling at McGrath's house one evening and asking why Dave had set up his own group rather than remain in Tara (by this time Dave had already told Molyneaux about McGrath's sexuality). As far as Garland recollects, McGrath gave an evasive answer, to the effect that he did not know why Dave had left Tara.

In spite of the stories now circulating, McGrath continued to gather around him a dedicated group of men who had genuine fears for the future of their country. More and more Dave began to feel that McGrath's band of young men simply repeated what he said, or what he told them to say. He often wondered if someone was manipulating McGrath. The thought also occurred to him that there might be someone on the Republican side manipulated by the same sinister force. Undaunted, later on, in 1971, Dave made an approach to another unionist politician,

Paisley, to share his concerns about McGrath, both sexual and political, but, according to Dave, he showed more interest in reassuring himself about four individuals in Tara who were also particularly close to him. Dave was frustrated once again. On a different occasion he approached another close unionist friend, the Reverend Robert Bradford, who had occasion to visit McGrath at his home. Disillusioned by the response of these influential figures, Dave soon abandoned the Orange Order and unionist politics.

Dave's attempts to expose McGrath as a homosexual hypocrite did not appear to deter the man himself. Fraser Agnew, who became an elected Ulster Unionist assemblyman for South Antrim (1982-86) and is currently a Newtownabbey Councillor, recalled his first meeting with McGrath in 1969 when he was chairman of the Young Unionist Council. The purpose of the meeting at McGrath's home in Wellington Park was, he told me during an interview in 1990, to receive information about the future and the problems which would lie ahead if O'Neill's policies were carried out. Agnew recalled the meeting:

> Even back in those days when we were not in the situation we were later to witness, Billy McGrath always believed there was going to be a final conflict where the Protestant/unionist/loyalist population should prepare for that final conflict. Not to involve themselves in any of the paramilitary activities we would see in later days, but simply to prepare for the final conflict. That was always his aim, his objective.

Clifford Smyth remembers that McGrath on the one hand wanted to direct his followers away from the path of violence. He told them not to get involved in the bloody civil disturbances and rioting because, as he put it, 'it will get much, much worse and we will all be required later to play a part in saving Ulster, at the point of a gun if necessary.' McGrath also insisted that the officers in Tara should not become involved in arms training because if Tara was investigated by the authorities, it was important that the officers were 'clean'. He wanted them to conceal documents as they travelled to and from meetings – meetings at which police files were available to help Tara develop its strategies.

4
'Doomsday' is Nigh

O'Neill's Prime Ministerial 'crossroads' broadcast soon led to what O'Neill described as the 'crossroads election' in February 1969. He was forced into this test of the electorate not only because of the disruption his reforms were causing within unionist circles, but also by the continuing violence which began in January with the ambush at Burntollet Bridge near Derry of a march organised by a radical left-wing group known as People's Democracy (PD).

Around forty marchers left Belfast on 1 January for a four-day walk to Derry, accompanied by twice as many police officers. All along their route the marchers were harried by loyalists and by the time of the Burntollet attack on 4 January their number had grown to several hundred. Without warning they were attacked by a crowd of more than two hundred loyalists wielding iron bars and sticks, and throwing bottles and stones. When the marchers finally reached Derry, the violence continued in the Bogside. In the first few weeks of 1969 more and more civil rights marches were organised in nationalist areas, with a corresponding rise in the number of Paisley-led counter-marches, and the Stormont Minister of Home Affairs was kept busy reviewing and banning the marches.

O'Neill continued to promote reforms, but to people like Paisley and McGrath these were merely concessions to the Catholic minority and they intensified their efforts to remove the Prime Minister from office. Recruitment drives drummed up increasing support for the UCDC and the UPV. McGrath continued to warn of an attempt by the civil rights movement to create the circumstances for constitutional change in Northern Ireland, claiming that it was a front for the IRA. Fraser Agnew and Clifford Smyth clearly remember the message from McGrath: 'Our enemies will make an attempt on the Northern Ireland state by a campaign which would represent the Stormont government to be a discredited government, backed by a discredited police force [the RUC].' Even as these early street disturbances took place, McGrath's standing in parts of the unionist community was greatly improved because when his followers recalled his predictions, they could not fail to be impressed by their accuracy.

By this stage McGrath's Orange ginger group, Tara, was beginning to attract more and more people from many walks of life. As Fraser Agnew recalled:

> I think this is how Billy McGrath always saw things. It was not a question of getting the masses out onto the streets and getting the masses to prepare ... no, it was getting at those who had influence in the community. Strangely enough, this is perhaps McGrath the enigma, because he was never at any stage one who held any position of authority either in the Orange Order or even in any of the unionist parties ... but yet he was able to wield an influence away from those organisations and he did it through organising these meetings under the guise of Tara.

McGrath had, of course, other means of exerting his influence, at one time being a delegate to the UUP and a branch member of the UUP. But he appears to have had a difficulty in belonging to any group which would have control over him: he never belonged to a particular church but set up his own evangelical organisation; he was not happy until he had established an Orange lodge of his own; and clearly he felt uncomfortable with the everyday politics of the unionist parties, preferring instead to create his own political talking-shop, Tara. However, after 1969, the character of Tara changed. McGrath began to forge closer links with the UVF and the masses were to become 'cannon fodder', as McGrath put it. He envisaged Tara as an evangelical elite directing operations under God.

Towards the end of January 1969 two members of O'Neill's government broke ranks and resigned. One was Brian Faulkner, the Deputy Prime Minister and Minister of Commerce, the other was William Morgan, the Minister of Health and Social Services, who was known to have attended prayer meetings in McGrath's home. (McGrath's brother Irwin worked for Morgan.) These resignations were quickly followed by a demand by twelve Unionist back-benchers for O'Neill's removal from office to keep the party united. A few days later, on 3 February, O'Neill announced the dissolution of parliament and called a general election, the 'crossroads election' for 24 February. In Bannside, O'Neill successfully defended his seat against Paisley (standing as a Protestant Unionist) and People's Democracy leader Michael Farrell. But even though the Unionist Party retained control of Parliament, there was still much confusion about who in the ruling party supported O'Neill's reforms and it soon became apparent that the divisions which existed before the election had not been healed. It was not much better on the streets. In the face of growing violence between civil rights protesters and the police, unionists of all shades began to succumb to a siege mentality. To a growing number of right-wing unionists, politics had failed and parades had failed. Encouraged by men like McGrath, there were those waiting in the wings to make their own arrangements to secure Northern Ireland's future by embarrassing and destabilising even further O'Neill's reforming government.

This was the year of the UVF bomb campaign, although some loyalists were prepared to point the finger of suspicion in another direction entirely, for reasons of political expediency. The Castlereagh electricity transformer was wrecked in a blast on 30 March and the following day Prime Minister O'Neill mobilised 1,000 members of the Ulster Special Constabulary (the 'B'-Specials) – a move of which McGrath approved because it dovetailed with his 'doomsday' plans. The bombings continued in April. On many occasions over the years I have heard Fraser Agnew and others tell the story about a meeting at McGrath's home (now in Greenwood Avenue on the Upper Newtownards Road). This was not a Tara meeting. The meeting was called late in the evening, Fraser believes a Saturday, just a few hours after one of the pipeline bombs exploded. Among those gathered in McGrath's home that night, according to him, were some individuals who then or later were prominent figures in unionist circles:

James Heyburn, a lifelong member of the Orange Order and fervent Paisley supporter who has served in a number of key positions for the DUP leader within the Free Presbyterian Church, such as treasurer and secretary. At present Worshipful Master of District Number 6.

David Browne, then deputy editor, later editor of Paisley's paper, the *Protestant Telegraph*.

Billy Douglas, a prominent figure in anti-Civil Rights demonstrations in South Derry during 1969 who was later an elected Ulster Unionist Councillor and assemblyman who briefly held office on a number of Assembly committees in the eighties.

Frank Millar Junior, Press Officer for the Young Unionist Council (1972-3); Research Officer for Ulster Unionist MPs at Westminster (1977-81); Press Officer at Unionist Party headquarters in Glengall Street, Belfast (1981-3) before becoming the Party's youngest ever General Secretary (1983-7). One of the three members of the unionist interparty task force set up to advise on tactics of opposition to the Anglo-Irish Agreement which was signed to huge unionist anger and street demonstrations in November 1985. Millar lived in McGrath's home for some time before marrying McGrath's daughter Elizabeth in January 1976.

Clifford Smyth, longtime friend of Paisley and prominent member of Paisley's political party, the DUP, prior to his expulsion in the mid-1970s. Graduate of Queen's. During student days chairman of the university's Conservative and Unionist Association (1971) and secretary of the Young Unionist Council. Elected DUP assemblyman in 1973-74. Close friend of McGrath for many years and described as the Intelligence Officer of Tara. He says his job was to provide an analysis of the political climate.

There were others present, but Agnew cannot identify those who were McGrath's family friends. According to him, McGrath told the hushed gathering the explosions were the work of a crack commando unit of the Éire Army, going as far as to name the man in charge as a Major Farrell. This unit had been specifically set up and trained with the aim of causing explosions which would shake O'Neill's government and pave the way for a small invasion force of Irish soldiers, thus creating the 'doomsday' scenario. During the meeting there was a telephone call for McGrath and as he left to take the call in the hallway, Agnew says Heyburn winked at Clifford Smyth and David Browne. Before the door closed they heard McGrath greet a unionist politician by name and say: 'Yes, everybody's here.' By the time this meeting was held, the *Protestant Telegraph* had (on 5 April), according to David Boulton in his book, *The UVF 1966–73* (Torc Books,1973), blamed the Castlereagh explosions on a splinter group of the IRA known as Saor Uladh, stating that the 'sheer professionalism of the act indicates the work of the well-equipped IRA ... '

However, Boulton points out that a month later, the *Protestant Telegraph* had taken a different tack altogether:

> A source close to government circles has informed us that the secret dossier on the Castlereagh electricity sub-station explosions contains startling documentation and facts. Original reports suggested that the IRA could have been responsible, but in parliament no such definite statement would be made ... We are told that the Ministry of Home

> Affairs is examining reports which implicate the Éire government in the £2 million act of sabotage... By actively precipitating a crisis in Ulster, the Éire government can make political capital, win or lose. The facts, we hope, will be made public thereby exposing the chicanery of the Dublin regime.

There is a striking similarity between this story and the one McGrath was telling those in his home that Saturday night. But it did not take Agnew long to discover who was really responsible for the bombings. The evening after this meeting (Sunday) he went with his girlfriend (now his wife) to the Ulster Hall in Belfast for one of Paisley's gatherings. As he arrived he was approached by a man who asked in a very excited tone what Agnew thought of the explosions. When Agnew related the story about Irish army involvement given out the night before by McGrath, the man became agitated and, taking him to one side, whispered: 'No, it was loyalists who did it.' The young Agnew was amazed, and as confused as he had been the night before when he asked McGrath to explain how such activities by the Irish army could in any way benefit the Dublin government. McGrath's response had a familiar ring: 'You never question the words of an intelligence officer!' Agnew told me it was the last night he ever attended meetings in McGrath's home, for the simple reason he was never invited back... although he later attended some meetings at Clifton Street Orange Hall.

O'Neill continued to push forward his reforms, securing the approval of his government on 23 April for universal adult suffrage in local government elections, thereby conceding the Civil Rights demand for 'one man, one vote'. But the resignation of the Agriculture Minister, Major James Chichester-Clark, once again highlighted the deep divisions the reform package created within the ruling party. The UVF response was swift. The next day an explosion shattered the main pipeline from Lough Neagh to Belfast and the following day another pipeline at Annalong in County Down. The bombs had the desired effect: three days later O'Neill resigned as Prime Minister, to be replaced on 1 May by Major Chichester-Clark. The political temperature was rising dramatically, street disorder was now virtually a daily occurrence and it appeared as if events were spinning rapidly out of the control not only of the police but also of the Stormont government.

Throughout the political turmoil, McGrath became a prolific letter-writer to news organisations and evangelical bodies all over the world, establishing important contacts in places as far apart as South Africa and Holland, mostly through the British Israelite movement. During the summer of 1969, McGrath decided he needed a printing machine to help with the growing demand for leaflets and flyers, so he bought a Rotaprint R75 on hire purchase. Paisley's church secretary James Heyburn and Roy Garland signed as guarantors for the hire-purchase price of £431, although with some misgivings on Garland's part.

By August 1969 the rioting reached such alarming levels, particularly in Derry, that the Republic's Taoiseach Jack Lynch made a television broadcast (13 August) announcing that field hospitals would be set up near the border:

> It is evident that the Stormont government is no longer in control of the situation. Indeed the present situation is the inevitable outcome of the policies pursued for decades by successive Stormont governments. It is clear also that the Irish government can no longer stand by and see innocent people injured and perhaps worse.

This speech appeared to support McGrath's claim that the Dublin government was plotting an invasion. Twenty-one years later, in 1990, one of the Dublin government ministers at the time, Neil Blaney, revealed that there *was* such a plan. In an interievw with *Hot Press* magazine in Dublin he confirmed that the Irish army was on standby to invade to cause what he described as an 'international incident'. Army units were sent to the border, he confirmed, in the guise of field hospitals, but the real intention was to invade Newry and Derry. The plan was circumvented by Lynch, he told the magazine, adding that during severe rioting in Ballymurphy, two Irish army trucks loaded with weapons and gas masks were dispatched to Belfast, but were stopped at Dundalk and 'were never seen again'.

Meanwhile Chichester-Clark was closely monitoring a deteriorating situation. The RUC was stretched to breaking point as it tried to deal with rioters in both communities; officers were exhausted after many days of long hours; and people living on either side of the religious divide were, for very different reasons, fearful of what lay ahead. As he watched developments from RUC headquarters in

Belfast, Chichester-Clark took time out to receive a delegation lead by Ian Paisley.

Roy Garland was invited to go along, and recalled the reason for the timing of Paisley's request to the Prime Minister to receive the delegation. It followed a meeting 'largely composed of members of Paisley's UCDC' in their offices at Shaftesbury Square. Paisley was in contact with the police and getting news of what was happening in different towns around the state. Then word came through that the Prime Minister would meet a delegation. Few were willing to travel to RUC headquarters, and it was because of this that Garland was asked to go along. This is how he described the meeting in *The Irish Times* of 14 April 1982:

> Many loyalists felt under threat during the violence of 1969 and it is not surprising that McGrath and Paisley were talking about the need for a 'People's Militia'. What is surprising is that at the height of this violence McGrath, Paisley, myself and a man called Black from Armagh were talking to the Prime Minister, Major James Chichester-Clark about it. This was during the early hours of Thursday, 14 August, 1969 at Knock RUC Headquarters. We were demanding that the 'B' Specials be mobilised and a 'People's Militia' be formed.

It seems the delegation made an immediate impact, for during the next twenty-four hours two important developments took place: all members of the 'B' Specials were told to report to the nearest police station and the British government agreed to a request from Northern Ireland to permit British soldiers to go on to the streets to assist the RUC. (Nationalist leaders also requested the intervention of the British army to protect their communities.)

Plans for a 'people's militia' to assist the security forces were taken a step further when Paisley organised a recruiting meeting at his old church on the Ravenhill Road in Belfast. Garland said he and McGrath, along with a few other men in Tara, patiently took down names and addresses, Paisley supervising the proceedings. Nothing much came of this effort, largely because many of the men had suspicions about McGrath. But not content to leave it at that, McGrath then turned to the Orange Order for assistance, addressing a meeting of leading Orangemen at Clifton Street Orange Hall, but his plea for help fell on deaf ears. At a meeting of Number 3 Belfast District of the Orange Order, a leading Orangeman asked McGrath and Garland why they did not just go ahead on their own.

Clifford Smyth recalls that hundreds of men answered the call to prepare for 'doomsday', and it soon became apparent that the UVF had joined en masse, swelling the ranks of Tara very rapidly indeed. In October 1969, another UVF bombing attack on an electricity sub-station at Ballyshannon in County Donegal went wrong. Thomas McDowell, a quarry foreman from Kilkeel in County Down, was injured when the bomb exploded and died in hospital before making any statement. Tara members marked the death by observing a minute's silence at a meeting. McDowell was a member of Mourne Free Presbyterian Church and of the South Down UPV. Gusty Spence was later to acknowledge McDowell as a UVF member who had died in action. McDowell died on 19 October, eight days after the first policeman of the Troubles was shot dead. Constable Victor Arbuckle died during two days of rioting on the Shankill Road following publication of the Hunt Report, which recommended replacement of the 'B' Specials, the establishment of a locally recruited regiment of the British Army and that the RUC become an unarmed civilian force.

In between these two deaths, on 14 October, McGrath attempted to use his growing influence to unite the unionist population:

> No word of mine is necessary to underline the gravity of the situation that now confronts the people of Northern Ireland. That this situation, with all its disastrous possibilities, is due to the lack of responsible political leadership is beyond doubt. The great and immediate need is for an overall political strategy that will embrace all the fragments of loyalist thought in our Province, and harness the total strength of our Protestant people for the great struggle for survival that lies before us. I have taken the responsibility therefore of calling together the following in the hope that in a private meeting such a strategy might be evolved:
>
> W. Black, Esq; D. Boal, MP; Reverend John Brown; Rt. Hon. W. Craig, MP; Reverend R. Dickinson, MA, BA; W. Douglas, JP; Dr N. D. Laird, MP; J. H. Molyneaux, Esq; Reverend I. R. K. Paisley, D. D; N. Porter, Esq; Reverend M. Smyth, B.A; H. West, MP.
>
> The above list includes many who in the past have been poles apart in their thinking and methods. It also includes many who because of person-

ality problems would in normal times find it difficult to work with others on the same list. These are not normal times and we should all be big enough to allow our differences, however legitimate, to be forged on the anvil of history into a weapon capable of defending the faith and freedom which we all profess to love.

I would be grateful therefore if you would let me know by return if you are willing to share in such a meeting as I suggest.

I remain,

Yours faithfully,

William McGrath

The attempt to convene the meeting failed. McGrath subsequently claimed to Garland that the meeting might have taken place but for the opposition of some of those invited. This caused it to be cancelled.

As 1969 drew to a close the sectarian mood worsened, with both communities feeling under threat, and in a development that was to have incalculable consequences for Northern Ireland, the Provisionals were born out of a split in the IRA. Meanwhile, back in Whitehall there was close scrutiny of how McGrath handled the situation on the ground. He was by now a very small wheel within a very big wheel, but with the help of elements of the British intelligence services he was about to play his part in changing for ever the face of politics on the Protestant-loyalist side of the sectarian divide.

5
'Our Heritage'

As the New Year of 1970 dawned on a troubled Northern Ireland, William McGrath was being guided by his handlers in MI5 as he made preparations for the next phase of the 'doomsday' plan. Tara had become a paramilitary group; recruitment had driven up the numbers and the organisation needed a new meeting place. As previously stated, Tara was not a paramilitary group in the way of other paramilitary organisations. In the twenty-five years of armed paramilitary conflict, not a single shot was ever fired in its name. Its members were to be left in a state of permanent readiness for a 'doomsday' scenario when law and order in the province would break down and Tara members would offer aid and assistance to the authorities in stabilising the situation. With a bit of persuasion McGrath got permission to use rooms at Clifton Street Orange Hall, although he was careful not to inform the Orange Order of the true nature of these meetings. Instead he got their approval for gatherings described to them as 'The Orange Discussion Group'. Now the serious business of recruiting and making plans for the 'doomsday' situation could begin, and McGrath undertook these tasks with gusto. The timing was just right to capture the mood of the unionist people, who viewed the growing disorder as an attack on their very right to exist.

As the number of Tara members grew rapidly into hundreds, McGrath was busy making preparations for a crucial element of his all-Ireland brand of Protestant evangelism. On 20 April 1970, a letter was sent to all members of St Mary's Church Men's Fellowship, Temperance LOL 1303, with some exciting news. It informed them:

> The Grand Orange Lodge of Ireland has agreed to the name of our Lodge being changed to 'Ireland's Heritage LOL 1303'. This decision has brought great joy to the Lodge, as it opens a new chapter filled with possibilities of service for our Institution and country.
>
> In order to cover the cost of our New Banner and other expenses, it will be necessary to raise at least £150. At our Lodge meeting it was proposed and adopted that each member be asked to raise at least £5 before the 12th July. This can be in the form of a personal subscription or collected from interested friends. Some members are hoping to sell pens and other items and so raise funds in this way. We know that we can depend on you to do your part.
>
> The Dedication of our new Banner, followed by a Dinner, will be held late in June or early in July, on a date to be decided later.
>
> Trusting you are in good health, and looking forward to seeing you at our next meeting.
>
> Yours in the cause of Protestantism,
>
> W. W. McGrath, Secretary.'
>
> [McGrath's son Worthington]

McGrath was already using a new Ireland's Heritage stamp on lodge correspondence – a harp with a crown perched on top, surrounded by shamrock and orange lilies.

According to members of Tara and the lodge, McGrath took great pride in marrying together symbols which were normally associated with sectarian opposites, especially in placing the crown of British Royalty above the harp of the Irish Republic.

Roy Garland was now McGrath's second in command in Tara and Clifford Smyth was the Intelligence Officer, with responsibility for providing an analysis of the volatile political situation. Frank Millar Junior and David Browne of the *Protestant Telegraph* were actively involved in Tara affairs at this early stage. Smyth and Garland were, on occasion, required to speak at meetings of the UVF, whose membership was very numerous in Tara. Among others who began to take a close interest in Tara was David Payne, a man later destined for notoriety as a tough UDA brigadier. The message McGrath communicated to them, and which they took back to their friends, colleagues and fellow travellers in the various organisations, was that Protestants should lay claim to what had once been theirs by right – the Irish culture, the Gaelic language. Part of the scenario was the removal of the Catholic Church from the reclaimed Protestant Irish State of the future, a position encapsulated in Tara literature by the catch-cry: *Tara – the hard core of Protestant resistance – resistance with responsibility! We hold Ulster that Ireland might be saved and that Britain be reborn.*

Before the end of April McGrath had an opportunity to reassert his stance on Catholicism when a fellow Orangeman transgressed – a sympathetic Unionist Party politician who had on occasion visited his home. Harry West, a future leader of his party and MP for Enniskillen from 1954 to 1972, received a letter from Ireland's Heritage Lodge on 25 April 1970, signed by McGrath's son, Worthington, and the Worshipful Master of the Lodge, Roy Garland, and forwarded to Worshipful Brother William Murdie, secretary of Number 3 District of the Orange Order:

> It is with deep sorrow of heart that we learn of the presence at a Romish Mass of our Brother, The Rt. Hon. Harry West, MP. That any member of our Order should offend in this way is a matter of great regret. That one such as Bro. West, who has served the cause so faithfully, should do so, underlines the necessity for each of us to seek a fuller understanding of the spiritual nature of the conflict in which our Institution is engaged and through which our Province is passing.
>
> Despite his proud record of service, we have no alterative but to call for the expulsion of Bro. The Rt. Hon. Harry West from our Institution in accordance with our Laws and Ordinances for this offence.

When it came to designing a banner for the new Ireland's Heritage Lodge, McGrath displayed the same quirky flair as in 1966, when Paisley's supporters marched through Belfast behind green-white-and-orange-coloured banners which McGrath had previously used in a 'holiness' campaign in the Republic. The new banner was certainly unique in the history of the Orange Order, for it included Gaelic inscriptions. One side showed the harp, adorned with the crown and the emblems of the four provinces,

Munster, Connacht, Leinster and Ulster – the old version of the nine-county Ulster flag, by now widely regarded as nationalist. The reverse side carried the same Irish language inscription, 'Oidhreacht Éireann', and a map of the thirty-two counties of Ireland with the crests of four cities, Londonderry, Belfast, Dublin and Cork. Underneath appeared in small lettering, 'Luke 19:13', and then in larger letters, 'Occupy till I Come'. Both sides were decorated with orange lilies; hanging from them were traditional Irish Celtic crosses, a design idea that came from Garland. Initially McGrath wanted the words on the banner to be: 'Again Boyne river shall flow blood red;/The heath be dipped in gore;/Ere Crownless harp in rebel hands shall fly o'er Ulster's shore.' Garland objected, as did Orange leader the Reverend Martin Smyth, and the idea was scrapped.

The unveiling ceremony was held in Belfast on 27 June. The event received much publicity and a photograph appeared in the *Belfast Telegraph*. Among those who availed of the photo opportunity around the new banner were Roy Garland, the Worshipful Master of LOL 1303, Walter Williams, Grand Secretary of the Grand Lodge of Ireland; John Bryans, Grand Master of Ireland and McGrath's former bible class teacher at North Belfast Mission on York Street. There was also Belfast County Grand Master, the Reverend Martin Smyth, who on this auspicious occasion performed the dedication of the new banner. All those present at the unveiling ceremony sang a hymn chosen by McGrath from his own hymn book. Garland was probably the only person present to realise that the words of 'Let me carry your Cross for Ireland, Lord,' were written by Thomas Ashe, an IRA hunger striker who died in a Dublin prison in 1917.

An Orange banner with a Gaelic inscription was a gift for the Irish government's public relations machinery. Just over a week after the unveiling of the banner, the Irish Minister for External Affairs, Dr Patrick Hillery, secretly visited Belfast for a tour of the Falls Road, a visit later denounced at Stormont by Prime Minister Chichester-Clark, who described it as a diplomatic discourtesy at a time of high tension. By now the Provisional IRA had embarked upon a bombing campaign aimed at setting the agenda for Catholic politics and at producing the environment for the collapse of the Stormont government, which they predicted would be the first step towards a united Ireland. The marching season approached and a massive contingent of police and soldiers was mobilised to prevent bloody disorder as 100,000 Orangemen took to the streets. In the event the parades, held in 1970 on Monday 13 July, passed off peacefully. 1970 marked the marching début of the Ireland's Heritage Lodge banner.

On the very day of the parades, Dublin's Department of External Affairs produced a bulletin containing the full text of an address to 'All Irish Traditions,' given on RTE on 11 July by the Taoiseach Jack Lynch, appealing to the better nature of people, North and South, Protestant and Catholic. The front cover featured the *Belfast Telegraph* photograph of the unveiling ceremony of the Ireland's Heritage Lodge banner. Someone sent a copy of the bulletin to the lodge and after discussion at a meeting it was decided to take this opportunity to make the government in Dublin fully aware of the history of the lodge and its aims. There was concern that the inclusion of Gaelic on the new banner was being represented as some kind of recognition of the Irish State by a group of Orangemen, but if that was the view in Dublin, Ireland's Heritage Lodge was quick to dispel any such notion in a letter to Dr Hillery, which was reproduced in the next bulletin from his department, along with his response.

Garland recalls that he offered to continue this correspondence with Dr Hillery but McGrath told him he would deal with it, although it appears there was no further contact between the two parties, perhaps because McGrath was preoccupied with Tara's affairs now that the recruitment programme had produced a marked increase in interest. However, he did not lose his desire to press ahead with his claims to an Irish identity for his members and within two years he had commissioned the design of four new standards for the Lodge, the four flags of the provinces – Munster, Connacht, Leinster and – of course – Ulster, once again using the colours normally associated with the nationalist Ulster flag. To mark the occasion, he found time to write a two-page leaflet setting out the aims of Ireland's Heritage under the rubric 'For the personal use of lodge members only'. It began:

> Political necessities over many generations have compelled the people of Northern Ireland to think of themselves as Ulstermen rather than Irishmen. This is the greatest tragedy of our history. If Ulster's story is glorious then Ireland's story is more glorious for the greater contains the lesser.

As 1970 drew to a close, McGrath's Tara group maintained its membership of hundreds from all over Northern Ireland. Those who joined did not take oaths but accepted the faith and freedom creed drafted by McGrath. He was against oaths because he insisted that Tara was not an organisation like other pseudo-paramilitary groupings (and it was never illegal); rather it had been established specifically for the 'doomsday' situation. It was McGrath's stated intention to have in place a disciplined group of dedicated men who would be ready to make the last stand for Ulster alongside the legitimate forces of law and order.

For the time being, it was sufficient to engage Tara members in discussion about how best they could defend their homeland against attack. The Clifton Street Orange Hall meetings – and similar meetings in many other halls throughout Northern Ireland – enabled members to air their concerns and offered them opportunities to hear lectures on how to defend themselves, as well as talks about how they should organise at street level in the event of a 'doomsday' scenario. According to Clifford Smyth, after Garland left, to be followed soon afterwards by the UVF membership, McGrath stressed at these meetings that there would be a spiral of violence in which the UVF would feed off the IRA and the IRA would feed off the UVF. The UVF had meanwhile been investigating detailed reports which they had received, and concluded that McGrath was working for Intelligence. Its members left Tara one night after a meeting in which McGrath was challenged by the UVF leader, 'Bo' McClelland. McClelland's questions were aimed at pressing McGrath into revealing whether or not he was homosexual. McGrath became embarrassed and responded by calling for McClelland to be 'drummed out'. The UVF leader stood up and called for his men to leave. They left, never to return.

McClelland and the UVF, from that time on, made it their business to hamper the work of Tara at every opportunity. McGrath, meanwhile, denounced the quality of loyalist leadership and the criminality of loyalist organisations. In public, at least, McGrath attempted to persuade his followers not to get involved in street skirmishes with the lawful authorities. But at the same time he was busy covertly gathering guns. These would be used in the 'doomsday' scenario.

It must here be emphasised that Tara was at no stage a proscribed organisation.

6
ON THE FRINGES

For William McGrath 1971 was a year of mixed fortunes. It was the year he was given his 'licence to seek thrills' – a job in Kincora working boys' hostel. It was the year his son Worthington got married, the year he briefly represented the Orange Order on the Unionist Council, but it was also the year his rapidly growing Tara organisation began to fall apart after the departure of the UVF. McGrath's standing in his new Orange Lodge was also temporarily damaged by revelations about his sexuality.

It was also a pivotal year for most people living in Northern Ireland. In 1971 the first British soldier died at gunpoint, signalling the start of the violent IRA campaign which was to continue for a quarter of a century. It was the year three Scottish soldiers were shot dead while having an off-duty drink in Ligoniel; it was the year of internment, of bomb attacks on the Four Step Bar on the Shankill and McGurk's Bar in the New Lodge area. It was also the year Ian Paisley and Desmond Boal announced the formation of a new political party, the Democratic Unionists and, perhaps most significantly, it was the year the UDA was officially formed following the distribution of leaflets in loyalist areas urging citizens to formalise their vigilante patrols into a properly constructed 'army'. These leaflets were handed out in loyalist areas of Belfast on 12 August, and in the Shankill Road area they were distributed at the height of serious rioting. Three writers on the Troubles have recognised the significance of this leaflet: David Boulton, in *The UVF 1966-73* (already cited) and Martin Dillon and Denis Lehane, in *Political Murder in Northern Ireland*, published by Penguin.

Dillon and Lehane describe the leaflet as the birth certificate of the UDA and reflect on the parallels to be drawn between the formation of the Provisional IRA on the Republican side and the creation of the UDA on the loyalist side. This is how the leaflet read:

> Being convinced that the enemies of the Faith and Freedom are determined to destroy the State of Northern Ireland and thereby enslave the people of God, we call on all members of our loyalist institutions, and other responsible citizens, to organise themselves immediately into platoons of twenty under the command of someone capable of acting as sergeant. Every effort must be made to arm these platoons, with whatever weapons are available. The first duty of each platoon will be to formulate a plan for the defence of its own street or road in cooperation with platoons in adjoining areas. A structure of command is already in existence and the various platoons will eventually be linked in a coordinated effort.
>
> Instructions: Under no circumstances must platoons come into conflict with Her Majesty's Forces or the Police. If through wrong Political direction Her Majesty's Forces are directed against loyalist people, members of Platoons must do everything possible to prevent a confrontation. We are loyalists, we are Queen's men! Our enemies are

> the forces of Romanism and Communism which must be destroyed.
>
> Members of platoons must act with the highest sense of responsibility and urgency in preparing our people for the full assault of the enemies within our province and the forces of the Éire government which will eventually be thrown against us. We must prepare now! This is total war!

The author of this piece was none other than William McGrath. The real significance of this development cannot be underestimated. Here we had a man under the ever-watchful control of MI5 writing a recruiting leaflet for an organisation which grew to be one of the most violent groups to operate during twenty-five bloody years in Northern Ireland. This was the man who was being carefully provided by British Intelligence with his 'special ability' to impress his followers that he could accurately predict the direction Northern Ireland would take through the maelstrom of violence and which – as he forecast – would include a strong element of tit-for-tat killing.

When it was confirmed to me in 1990 that McGrath was a small part of a much larger MI5 operation, I began to understand the true importance of his role in helping to create the climate for the establishment of the Ulster Defence Association. It seems clear that British Intelligence was using McGrath in its efforts to control loyalist counter-terrorism. McGrath often travelled to London to meet his contacts, referring to these trips as necessary gatherings of the 'Belfast–London' committee. Clifford Smyth and Roy Garland remember that McGrath would inform Tara members that those he met in London were influential friends of Northern Ireland who were watching McGrath's group of young, middle-class, well educated unionists develop and who would be there to help them in achieving political success.

If McGrath was to continue to make an impact on loyalist-unionist thinking during these years of the early 1970s, he would have to survive the whispering campaign which was by now gathering momentum. Dave was still speaking to leading unionist figures about McGrath's homosexuality and he says that it was during this year that he spoke to Paisley. There was also growing tension between McGrath and his second-in-command, Roy Garland. According to Garland, McGrathintroduced a command structure to Tara. The title of Officer Commanding (OC) he assigned to himself. The membership was divided into groups of 'platoons', headed by 'sergeants'. Monthly meetings were attended by the heads of individual platoons. Garland has described his duties as McGrath's deputy, which included ensuring that the monthly meetings were called to order before the 'entrance' of the OC McGrath. Each gathering started with a ritual statement about Tara's part in the struggle for the soul of Ireland. The meetings would be attended by the 'sergeants' of all the 'platoons'. New sergeants were initiated, new members admitted. Most new members did not return to this monthly meeting as it was intended only for platoon leaders. Each platoon was responsible for running its own affairs.

There was one intriguing interlude during these early days of Tara meetings when a stranger turned up for a meeting. This man was on his first mission for MI5, having been told to penetrate this new Tara group and if possible Ireland's Heritage Lodge. But at the first meeting of Tara he attended he was singled out as an agent by a member of the UVF, who approached Garland to tell him about the interloper. Garland informed McGrath, who instructed his second-in-command to escort the man from the building. Garland said he led him out of the meeting and left him standing at the door of Clifton Street Orange Hall. In 1990, I travelled to England and met this man, who told me his handlers did not seem too disappointed that he had been detected and told him to forget all about Tara and McGrath. He did manage to gather some information but when he tried to pass it on to his handlers they repeated their insistence that he forget all about McGrath and Tara. From that time on, he was forbidden to mention Tara, McGrath or Ireland's Heritage, although he was never told why. Over the years, this man was not the only 'British' agent to take an interest in McGrath and Tara, nor was he alone in finding his intelligence unexpectedly rejected by those in higher authority.

By now the relationship between Garland and McGrath had deteriorated on a number of levels – in business, in matters relating to sex and to religious teaching. Garland was having difficulty accepting McGrath's rejection of civil and religious liberty for all, which Garland had been taught to respect in the small mission he had attended from childhood. He now saw that McGrath was prepared to deny freedom to Protestants who did not share his views. In business terms, Garland's accountant informed him that he was being fleeced by McGrath, who received a monthly sum from Garland by way of a convenant to the Christian

Fellowship Centre but had borrowed other amounts, as well as being permitted for a time by Garland to use his name for credit in running his carpet import business. Garland eventually had to sue McGrath to secure the £1,300 owed to him. Of course, by now Garland had had his suspicions about McGrath's homosexuality confirmed by a number of young men who said that McGrath had sexually abused them.

As Garland told *The Irish Times* in 1982, McGrath preached the highest standards of relationships between men and women, which meant no sex before marriage. At the same time, he tried to promote physical love between men as not only permissible but desirable. 'I realised when he [McGrath] said I had an 'emotional block',' Garland told the Dublin newspaper, 'this simply meant that I could not take part in homosexual activities. Even at this stage it was impossible to be sure, because he had always denied being a homosexual and he even condemned homosexual activity. In the early days of his 'ministry' he said it was part of his 'ministry' to help homosexuals with their problems. Had this been true I would have supported him, but I found no evidence of it.'

McGrath was secretly having sexual relationships with men but without the cooperation of any of his sexual partners, it is difficult to establish exactly who was involved. There is absolutely no suggestion that any members of Tara other than McGrath were involved in homosexual activity. Most were amazed and shocked when the truth became known. However, there were various known homosexuals involved in McGrath's political life at the time, some with very interesting connections.

In the volatile political climate of the early 1970s, a number of figures would briefly dominate events in their own areas, earning notoriety as back-street generals. One such figure was the leader of the Shankill Defence Association, John McKeague, who later became leader of the vicious Red Hand Commandos. (The INLA claimed responsibility for the murder of McKeague in 1982.) He was known to the police as someone with a sexual appetite for young boys but he was also an active homosexual and he was known to visit McGrath at Kincora. During a visit to the Maze Prison I met a prisoner on a loyalist wing who recalled being with McKeague one evening when they drove together to Kincora and went inside for a conversation with McGrath. McKeague and McGrath were trying to arrange some exchange of weapons.

There were other important people on the fringes of McGrath's life at this time. Several people who were members of Tara in the mid-1970s told me that McGrath was in regular receipt of funding from a secret source, which they discovered to be Sir Knox Cunningham, who died on 29 July 1976. A glance through *Who's Who* reveals that Sir Knox was a leading figure in the Orange Order, an Apprentice Boy of Derry, Provincial Grand Master of the Masonic Province of Gloucester, member of the Ulster Unionist Council from 1943; on the National Executive of the Conservative Party 1959–1966; Freeman of London 1956; served in the Scots Guards during the Second World War; Ulster Unionist Westminster MP for Antrim South from 1955–70. When he gave up the seat in 1970, it was his election agent James Molyneaux who took over, to begin a long career in politics which culminated in his leadership of the Ulster Unionists and membership of the Westminster Privy Council. Sir Knox Cunningham had an extremely long and distinguished career in parliament, which peaked in the period 1959-63 when he was the Parliamentary Private Secretary to Prime Minister Harold Macmillan. The most interesting entry in *Who's Who* reveals that he studied at Fettes Clare College in Cambridge, where he was heavyweight boxing champion in 1931. A Cambridge contemporary was one of Knox Cunningham's closest friends, Sir Anthony Blunt, the Keeper of Her Majesty the Queen's pictures, the epitome of the British establishment, who finally confessed in 1979 that he had been a Soviet agent.

The Blunt connection with Northern Ireland does not end there, for also at Cambridge during the Soviet spy's days was another member of the Northern Ireland aristocracy, Peter Montgomery [now deceased]. The family home was at Blessingbourne estate, Fivemiletown. He was born in the same year as Knox Cunningham (1909), second son of Major-General Hugh Maude de Fellenberg Montgomery; his uncle was Field Marshal Sir Archibald Montgomery-Massingberd and his second cousin was the legendary Second World War commander. Montgomery and Blunt became lovers but when the affair had run its course they remained lifelong friends. While they were at Cambridge, Montgomery was unaware that so many of his close friends were spying for the Soviet Union, although he himself was to become involved in British Intelligence when during the Second World War he was a captain in the Royal Intelligence Corps. In 1945 he was made ADC to the Viceroy of India, Earl Wavell. After that he became more deeply involved in Northern Irish affairs, serving on the BBC's advisory council from 1952-71 and spending a year on the Board of Visitors at Her Majesty's Prison, Belfast. He served on the board of the Northern Ireland Arts Council, of which he was president from 1964-74, in 1964 became the High Sheriff of County Tyrone, and later Her Majesty's Vice-Lieutenant of the same county (1971-79). It is easy to understand why such an 'establishment' figure feared discovery as a homosexual.

The key to the activities of this particular group lies with Robin Bryans, a Northern Ireland born author who wrote prolifically under the pseudonym Robert Harbinson. He is a cousin of John Bryans, the leading figure in the Orange Order who became the Grand Master of Ireland, who was McGrath's bible study teacher at the North Belfast Mission in the York Street area and who later attended prayer meetings and British Israelite meetings in McGrath's home.

In 1990 I had a number of long telephone conversations with Robin Bryans [hereafter referred to as Harbinson] and eventually went to his West Ealing home in London to meet him in May of that year. Throughout our conversation he frequently referred to his Orange Order relative John as 'bible Jack', informing me that Blunt's nickname for his brother was 'Hellfire Jack'. Harbinson reeled off names of people prominent in Northern Irish and British establishment circles at such speed that it was difficult to keep track of the sequence of events and the connections he was describing. However, once I returned to the office and typed up my notes, it was possible to cross-check some of what he had told me with what had already been related in a number of books about Blunt, about other Cambridge graduates such as Kim Philby, Donald Maclean, Guy Burgess; and about the intelligence battle between MI5 and the KGB during the 'Cold War' years.

Harbinson had one interesting tale to tell about Blunt and Montgomery during the Second World War. He says that in 1942 Blunt rushed to Northern Ireland on what he described at the time as a 'mercy mission' to help solve some difficulty Montgomery faced at his home in Fivemiletown. Montgomery was a regular visitor to Blunt's apartment in London; indeed there was a spare room permanently ready to accommodate him even when Blunt lived with another of his Northern Ireland lovers. When Blunt made his 'mercy' mission visit, remember that Britain was at war and Montgomery was a captain in Intelligence, while Blunt was a Soviet spy, although this was not to emerge for many years. Another frequent visitor to Blunt's home was Sir Knox, described by Harbinson as a 'muffle queen' who liked to be 'screwed by young boys'. Given Knox Cunningham's knowledge of Tara and McGrath, and given that McGrath made visits to London for meetings of the 'Belfast-London' committee, it is just possible that Knox Cunningham was able to introduce his acquaintance McGrath to his London friends, such as Montgomery, Blunt and others, including a man who held a senior post in the Northern Ireland office in Belfast in the mid seventies, P. T. E. England, Peter to his friends. Harbinson knew Peter England and his family in Surrey very well indeed and he was aware that England was under suspicion during his two years in Northern Ireland (1974-76) because of his sexuality.

According to Harbinson, Blunt was well known in the

gay community as someone who enjoyed a bit of 'rough trade', so it was not uncommon for him to have young boys call at his apartment for sexual congress. For his visits to Northern Ireland, Blunt knew someone who could supply the 'rough trade', although on occasion, according to Harbinson, he was forced to seek help from Montgomery who was not, again according to Harbinson, interested in young boys. Both Montgomery and Blunt had contacts within the Royal Family – Blunt's obviously through his work for the Queen and Montgomery through his friendship with a family in Enniskillen. Harbinson said Lord Mountbatten would visit this family on his way to his boat on the other side of the border at Mullaghmore in County Sligo. Here he spent every August for thirty years with members of his family until he was murdered by the IRA on 27 August 1979. His fourteen-year old grandson Nicholas and a fourteen- year old crew member from Enniskillen, Paul Maxwell, also died in the radio-triggered explosion. The Dowager Lady Brabourne died later from her injuries.

In April 1990 Harbinson stated publicly in the Dublin-based magazine *Now* that Lord Mountbatten, Montgomery, Blunt and England were all involved 'in an old-boy network which held gay orgies in country houses and castles on both sides of the Irish border.' Harbinson told me in the course of a telephone conversation in January 1990 that he had written letters in the early 1970s to various people in authority in London about the child sex abuse going on in Northern Ireland – although he did not mention Kincora. He was moved to write these letters because of the anger he felt about the blackmail of a Belfast homosexual by a former lover, described by Harbinson in these letters as a 'male prostitute'. Apparently the wealthy Belfastman offered to reach a financial settlement with his lover when the relationship ended but the lover wanted double the £500,000 on offer. The ex-lover then became a menace to the married Belfastman, making threatening noises and demanding the full million pounds settlement. His behaviour outraged Harbinson and when his early letters were ignored he began to campaign very actively, sending letters and postcards to the rich and powerful in British establishment circles. Once the postcards began to circulate there were complaints to the police and Harbinson was warned that he would be prosecuted for criminal libel. Harbinson says the police officer in charge of the case was from the Sussex Constabulary – a man by the name of George Terry, who would eventually be called in to investigate the Kincora case in the early 1980s.

Harbinson's claims paint an intriguing picture! Together with the testimony of others who knew McGrath, they provide strong evidence that the OC of Tara was at the very least on the fringes of this British establishment group.

Part III
Kincora 1958–71

7
A Home from Home

Hugh Quinn spent his whole childhood in care, having been abandoned by his mother at birth because she thought he stood a better chance in public care than with her in poverty. His memories of an upbringing in institutions of the state are horrific. There was little love or affection in a system which victimised those least able to speak up for themselves. By the time he reached Kincora he had already endured abuse, although it did not prepare him for what lay ahead.

Quinn was born on 13 December 1945, in a workhouse on the Lisburn Road in Belfast, a site now occupied by the City Hospital. 'My mother abandoned me at the workhouse,' he recalled. 'She simply could not afford a home for us. When the workhouse disappeared in 1948 with the introduction of the National Health Service, I was placed in a home called Bawnmore. It was marvellous and the matron at the home was Mrs [Minnie] Wilson, the one person I grew to love and trust. She became my mother figure.' But his contentment was not to last. Hugh was moved several times to other institutions.

'During my stay in one particular home I developed temper tantrums, which resulted in the decision to move me to Kincora, even though I was younger than the other boys. It was thought that Joe Mains could control me.' From his very first day in Kincora, Quinn was to discover the type of control Mains would establish over him:

> I remember the first day I arrived at Kincora. Joe Mains took me to the bathroom. He told me to strip naked and he gave me what he called a medical examination. This entailed him putting his hand around my testicles and asking me to cough. At one point he said: 'Aren't you a big boy for your age?' When he said this he was looking at my penis. I was embarrassed. Later he invited me to his bedroom. Under threat of sending me to borstal he forced me to masturbate him and kiss him on the lips. Soon he started asking me to have anal sex with him. During the next three years he had intercourse with me once or twice a week. I was fourteen when this happened. I was an orphan from birth and by this stage I was institutionalised. I could not bring myself to complain about Mains because he was such a highly regarded person who told me that no one would believe me and if I created trouble I could be sent to borstal. I had no family . . . the people at Kincora were the closest I had to family.

Hugh Quinn lived in Kincora from 1960 to 1964.

From the very first day it was opened by Belfast Welfare Authority in 1958, the Kincora Working Boys' Hostel provided its paederast warden Joe Mains with a constant supply of young boys. The large detached villa at 236 Upper Newtownards Road in East Belfast had once known happier times as a family home. Now its role was to provide a homely, caring environment for deprived teenagers – a stable background to aid the difficult transition from boyhood to manhood. Kincora was to offer accommodation to a maximum of twelve boys in the fifteen-eighteen age group, boys from unfortunate family backgrounds or broken homes or who had been orphaned by the sudden loss of both parents. Given the location of the hostel in East Belfast, most of those taken into care and placed there were Protestants.

Joseph Mains got the job as warden in charge of the hostel after a succession of other assignments with Belfast Welfare Authority. He was twenty-six years old at the time, he was single and had some previous experience as warden of a boys' home. His personnel file was made public during the Hughes Enquiry in 1984 and the records revealed that he had experience in nursing and in voluntary youth work. Those same files do shed a little light on how a man so apparently poorly qualified to manage a hostel for boys managed to obtain this position with the welfare authority. There was a shortage of qualified staff to fill positions such as these at the time. I quote from the official records: 'The Ministry of Home Affairs Inspector, who knew him [Mains] from his earlier childcare work, was complimentary in recommending that his appointment to Kincora be approved by the Ministry.'

Mains took up his post in March 1958 and although the official opening of Kincora did not take place until May of that year, a number of boys were already in residence by the time the civic dignitaries arrived to join in the celebrations. The city fathers, councillors and aldermen, brushed shoulders with health officials, social service staff and the young residents of Kincora, who passed around tea and cakes. Mains had managed to fool his employers but the first boys to be placed in Kincora knew the truth. From day one Mains revealed himself to them as a paederast.

Passing round sandwiches and sticky buns to councillors, doctors, social workers, politicians and VIPs from all walks of life was something Hugh Quinn grew to dislike intensely during his four-year stay at Kincora. At Christmas and holiday times such professionals visited the hostel, and throughout the year there were unscheduled visits from various people with an interest in social services or in the hostel residents. 'On these occasions,' said Quinn, 'if we were at the house, we would be expected to carry tea and biscuits to the guests. It really was sickening. Sometimes police officers would call in for a chat with Mains or other members of the staff. I thought of crying out and telling them everything, but Mains was careful to make sure he was always hanging around and I was frightened that if I did and no one believed me I would be in serious trouble with Mains.'

Quinn acknowledges that the sexual favours provided for Mains bought certain privileges. But he is also sure he was not alone in being asked to provide them. On the nights he did not sleep with Mains in the warden's private accommodation, the ground floor apartment at the rear of the house, others did. Quinn saw Mains collect them from the dormitory upstairs. For those who complied with Mains wishes and did not kick up a fuss, there were trips to the theatre, to bars and clubs. Even driving lessons were offered as rewards. Quinn was taken to places where homosexuals gathered clandestinely at the time, the early 1960s. 'There was the Queenscourt Hotel in Bangor where we were brought many times. I remember on one occasion I was introduced to pop singer Eden Kane, who was performing at the hotel at the time. Sometimes Mains, who was bisexual, would bring his girlfriend on these trips and we would go to dances together, but most of the time we were in the company of gays.' (Mains's girlfriend was completely unaware of his sexual leanings.) Other venues described by Quinn as homosexual haunts were Matthew's Café in Belfast city centre and the Royal Avenue Bar at the Avenue Hotel. Quinn recalled: 'He would take me there to meet other gays. Mains knew the comedian James Young very well and Jack Hudson, Young's partner and mentor. I was often in their company and we got tickets for the show and were permitted to go backstage afterwards.'

Mains was so confident of his control over Quinn that he took him to meet not just other homosexuals but his own relatives and friends. One relative was a senior policeman. He was ignorant of Mains's activities. On such visits Quinn briefly entertained thoughts of telling him that Mains's was sexually abusing boys at the hostel but the fear of not being believed quickly drove such thoughts away.

Given Quinn's early introduction to homosexuality it is perhaps not surprising that he blames his treatment at Kincora for his own sexual orientation. 'I had relationships with girls,' he said sourly, 'but I found I was incapable of maintaining a relationship and ended up seeking the company of other men. I was even engaged to be married once but could not go through with it. How would my wife react when I told her about my past and what about children in the future. The truth is that Joe Mains made a mess of my life.'

If Mains's appointment as warden was mystifying, the choice of his deputy was positively bizarre. Raymond Semple, a single man of forty-two, was brought into the Kincora fold in September 1964 and as police records show, within a matter of days he had forced himself sexually on one of the residents, a boy who had already been abused by Mains. The boy soon found himself providing sexual favours for both the warden and his deputy. Although the job specification clearly stated that preference would be given to 'applicants who have a working knowledge of the running of a children's home', Semple, the successful candidate, had no such knowledge.

When Semple left school in 1938, he joined the workforce at Harland and Wolff's shipyard in east Belfast as a fitter's helper, a position he held until after the Second World War. Then he spent two years with Shorts aircraft company before returning to his old job at the shipyard. His decision to apply for the job was prompted by his close friend and fellow homosexual, Joe Mains. According to Semple, Mains told him there was 'a job coming up' for which he should apply. Mains and Semple had become close friends through their mutual interest in the St John's Ambulance Brigade; Semple had spent twenty-five years with the service. There is little chance that Semple's application would have succeeded without the support of his friend Mains, coupled with the fact that there was a serious shortage of qualified staff at the time. An official investigation into Semple's appointment at Kincora concluded thus: 'Mr Semple had no relevant previous employment or social work qualification but had been working in Kincora on a voluntary basis for three years and was, like Mr Mains, associated with St John Ambulance Brigade. In retrospect it may just be possible to feel some uneasiness in the fact that both Mr Mains and Mr Semple were single, were known to each other and that Mr Mains acted as referee for Mr Semple in his application for a post involving the care of teenage boys.' Throughout the 1960s, therefore, Kincora was being run by two active paederasts.

The fact that these abuses continued over a period of twenty years, apparently undetected, might tend to suggest that the abused had suffered in silence. This would be an erroneous conclusion. There were complaints to social workers, to staff at the head office of social services in Belfast and in a letter to a Belfast police station. In their ignorance of the full facts, some boys turned to the head of the hostel, Joe Mains, seeking comfort and help to end the abuses, initially by Semple but later by McGrath. One resident who complained to Mains about Semple between 1964 and 1966 was later to tell an enquiry: 'At the time, of course, I did not know about Mains. I did not know he too was involved in sexual assaults on other residents. Mains listened to my complaint and told me he would speak to Semple and tell him to stop it.'

I traced former Kincora residents. As many had built new lives far removed from the bitter experiences inside the hostel my approaches had to be made with tact. But many of them seemed relieved finally to discover someone who was prepared to listen and give the oxygen of publicity to their painful plight. While Hugh Quinn was happy to be identified, most others, understandably, requested anonymity. I have concealed the identities of those whose statements to the police I have studied.

An examination of the lengthy catalogue of cries for help made during the 1960s reveals Mains's *modus operandi*. Unlike the other members of staff, Mains lived on the premises. He had a self-contained apartment at the rear of Kincora which could be entered from inside the hostel but which also had a separate entrance off North Road. Having singled one of the boys out for his special attention, Mains would use his authority to find out if the individual concerned would offer strong resistance or not. The first officially recorded complaints were made in September 1967 and perfectly illustrate his methods, for there were other similar complaints in later years. They were lodged by two Kincora residents at the headquarters of the Belfast Welfare Authority in College Street and comprised written statements against the warden.

One of the accusers said Mains had felt all over his body, put his hands down his underpants during a summer camp and asked, 'Do I get a kiss then?' when the boy was washing. The other boy complained that Mains told him he was 'lovely' when he was having a bath and later turned up in the boy's room, where he put his hands under the bedclothes and felt his body all over. These written statements were passed on to Henry Mason, the City Welfare Officer at the time, and on 8 September 1967, Mr Mason interviewed Joe Mains at some length, considered Mains's explanations and judged them 'plausible'. Mains said he had put his hands down the boy's pants because the individual concerned 'was inclined not to change his underclothes', frequently keeping the clean set in his locker. On the question of asking for a kiss, Mains said this was an attempt to shame the boy into getting his long hair cut and he admitted using the same question in an attempt to embarrass the other boy. Henry Mason's conclusion must be put in the context of the period. Given that it is only in recent years that society has come to terms with the reality of sexual abuse in state institutions, his conclusion was not surprising and it would be difficult to fault it. He was later to tell a committee of enquiry that he did not at the time consider the matter closed and agreed with hindsight that the truth of the allegations that Mains was a homosexual should have been established one way or the other.

Mason forwarded his report to the Town Clerk with his conclusion that there was no evidence to constitute a '*prima facie* indication of wrongful conduct'. He recommended that the social worker who took the statements from the boys speak to them again and explain to them the reasons for the incidents. There were two other recommendations: that there should be a closer supervision of Kincora and that there should be a careful sifting of any further information 'coming our way'. It was to be some four years before the 'Mason file' was to be resurrected, on the occasion of another complaint from a Kincora resident who wrote to the health authorities and to the police. The allegations this time were that Mains had paid the boy five shillings (25p) to rub oil into his back and made grunting noises in satisfaction. Further, the boy alleged, Mains persuaded him to sleep in his private quarters one night, during which time Mains had put his arms around him muttering, 'On to it, on to it.'

Henry Mason sent details of this second complaint, as well as his records of the 1967 complaints, to the Town Solicitor, John A. Young, on 21 August 1971. But it seems the file disappeared with no evidence of any response, let alone action from the Town Solicitor's office. Indeed there may be a very simple explanation for this apparent 'inaction' on the part of the Town Solicitor. The late John Young was a practising homosexual, active in a small coterie of men which included Joe Mains. As the police were to discover, the third member of this group was a Unionist Councillor, Joshua 'Joss' Cardwell.

With John Young, Semple and Mains formed a homosexual triumvirate that was undoubtedly able to keep complaints from the young male residents under wraps, at the same time safeguarding its own dark secret. The 1971 complaint again revealed Mains's methods of sounding out potential sexual conquests. On this occasion the young man managed under extreme duress to maintain his strength and reject Mains's sexual advances. But Hugh Quinn was not the only resident over the years to fall under the influence of Mains who, as Quinn has testified, had a girlfriend as part of his cover. On occasion Mains would take one of the young Kincora residents to his girlfriend's house to get help with gardening chores. One resident was asked if he wanted to stay for the night at Mains's girlfriend's house. That night, according to the young man, as the girlfriend slept upstairs, Mains had sex with him in the living room below.

In spite of the growing number of complaints against him, Mains managed to keep his job and clearly still enjoyed the trust of his employers. He was able to give 'plausible' explanations for those complaints which could not be stifled by his influential friends. Later, the Sir George Terry enquiry criticised the police for not acting on early reports of abuses in Kincora. The Hughes Report was similarly critical of the role of the social services. Mains and Semple might have continued to get away with their crimes for many more years but for the employment in 1971 of a new member of staff, house father William McGrath. It was McGrath's arrival in August which produced a very marked increase in the frequency of complaints, and perhaps more importantly, the nature of the complaints. The approaches to the boys made by Mains and Semple were initially subtle. They 'tested' the resistance of those they targeted and if the will was strong enough to reject their advances, the individuals concerned would be left alone. But William McGrath's methods were much more direct and were applied with a strong degree of menace and force. McGrath's forceful approach upset the balance at Kincora and ultimately the volume of complaints grew so alarmingly as to bring about the disclosures which eventually resulted in jail sentences for all three Kincora staff – and for three other men involved in the same kind of activity at other public institutions.

The beast of Kincora had arrived.

8
ENTER THE BEAST

Kincora was like a haunted house as I walked around inside on that cold January night in 1982. It was as if I were not alone, as if I had for company the lost souls of those who had once lived there. The statements made by the residents which I had read and the reports of the investigating policemen were brought chillingly home to me. Some forensic scientist or RUC scene-of-crime officer had the unpleasant task of searching out clues from the carpets covering the stairs and landings, to establish the veracity of the statements made by former residents. The fact that the investigators found traces of semen on the floor-covering in the hallway, the landings and the stairs – not what one would normally expect – bore testament to the claims made by the young men once incarcerated there.

McGrath's appetite for these young men was insatiable, and it was quite clear from statements and interviews given to police that he was not always the gentle seducer. In the toilet on the landing McGrath had raped a young boy – we will call him Sammy to protect his true identity – on his final day in the hostel, as foster parents waited downstairs to take him to a new home. In the same toilet McGrath had raped the boy in on his first few days at Kincora. Sammy's description of his brief spell in Kincora was undoubtedly the principal reason detectives nicknamed McGrath 'The Beast'.

Sammy came from a broken home. From the time his

mother left when he was twelve, he had experience of different residential homes, as he was moved from one to another in the Belfast area for the next four years. Sammy's statement that he had repeatedly been raped by McGrath was eventually used to confront the 'Beast'. It was the basis of charges to which McGrath eventually pleaded guilty, thereby removing any possibility that his evidence would be heard in open court.

Sammy's years in different institutions had taught him to respect house masters. He says he did once tell one of the many social workers he had to deal with, but that she just laughed, as McGrath told him 'they' would if he dared to speak out. In spite of her reservations, the social worker did raise Sammy's complaint with Mains and McGrath. Sammy was called in after they had time to discuss his allegations, to hear McGrath describe him as a liar in front of Mains and the social worker and to see Mains turn his back on him. By this stage, the mid-1970s, there had already been complaints against McGrath, including Garland's anonymous call to Strandtown RUC station. Garland alleged that boys at the home were being abused.

Mains felt a great dislike for McGrath from the moment he arrived unannounced at the front door of Number 236 Upper Newtownards Road in June 1971. Raymond Semple recalled his surprise and anger. Apparently Mains had not been consulted about the appointment of McGrath; indeed Semple claimed that he and Mains simply did not know of any plan to fill a third staff position at the hostel. But once they checked with the Director of Social Services they realised that McGrath's appointment was a *fait accompli*. No one has any idea why McGrath took this job in Kincora.

He certainly had no formal qualifications. It may have been an attempt to stabilise his family's income. Apparently two clergymen, who have never been identified, provided references for him.

Even with Sammy, McGrath boasted about his contacts 'high up in the Orange Order and in loyalist paramilitary groups like the UDA as well as politicians such as Paisley'. Sammy remembers McGrath's boast that during the 1974 loyalist strike he was involved in talks with representatives of the Northern Ireland Office. McGrath did mention Tara to Sammy, asking one day if he had ever heard of the group, then explaining the name of the organisation as 'something to do with the Free State'. At this point, according to Sammy, McGrath burst out laughing and said there was more to the word Tara than he could ever begin to understand. He said it was part of the Orange Order, but a part of the Order made up of Protestants who thought differently from the rest of the Orange Order, people who believed that Catholics should have no say in society.

McGrath would test the boys politically as they watched the news on television, and occasionally if he was satisfied that the person concerned was a Protestant with strong anti-Catholic views he might be invited to consider membership of Tara. Sammy remembers that some of the boys living in Kincora were involved with loyalist paramilitary groups, occasionally the UVF but mostly the UDA. During a television interview in 1990 I asked him if there had ever been any evidence of weapons in the house, because another former Kincora resident I had traced to London in 1982 told me that on one occasion he saw one of the boys with a gun. Sammy said he was never aware of any guns in the home although boys did boast about having weapons. I then asked him if there was anyone he could think of at Kincora who was definitely actively involved in paramilitary organisations? He answered:

> There was one lad whose name I forget and he came in one night very late and McGrath was on duty, he was in the building anyway. It was very unusual to see him [McGrath] in the building at that time of night and the boy came in. He was in the same room as me but I cannot remember his name. He was a lad for talking, though, and he was shaking a bit. His clothes were all gathered up and McGrath took them all out and one of the lads asked him what was up, so he turned round and says he was just after shooting someone. And we tried to ask him, a couple of us, who it was, but before we could get any more information McGrath just came in and told us to shut up. I think he started waiting a bit, outside the door listening, so we just shut up and next morning there was not anything mentioned. The lad just said nothing about it. That is the only really serious time.

And in answer to a question about what happened to the clothes?

> McGrath took them outside. There was a kind of big thing . . . just seen the light like, coming up and this . . . he burned them because we never seen

them. So he did not like... there was a laundry room downstairs and they were not in that like... so we assumed he burned them.

There may have been another explanation for the boy's behaviour that night, but Sammy and the others believed that his physical state, 'the shaking', was evidence of a serious occurrence. There were others during this period of the mid-1970s who observed the gun-running McGrath, and even some who knew of his association with loyalist hardliners like John McKeague, who also had a taste for young boys. For Sammy it was a reminder that McGrath had contacts on the outside and that if there was going to be any trouble he had a means of dealing with it. It certainly discouraged Sammy from reporting McGrath, so he continued to force his unwanted attentions on the boy.

Mains was undoubtedly uncomfortable with McGrath but he also had selfish reasons for wishing to keep a lid on McGrath's growing catalogue of abuses. The level of complaints mushroomed once McGrath took up his post. Indeed, one of the most bizarre comments came from Semple, who told police during questioning: 'Because of the amount of complaints made to me and Mains about McGrath interfering with the residents me and Mains tried to watch McGrath. I could not find out anything while I was on duty. There was plenty of talk about McGrath interfering with the boys by the boys but I could not find out anything.' There is no evidence to show that Mains and Semple advanced these complaints about McGrath through the proper channels.

I paused briefly in the office. There was still a desk, a couple of chairs, a calendar on the wall and a filing cabinet. I tugged at one of the drawers on the cabinet. The most important files had long since been removed, no doubt by the police seeking clues as to the identity and whereabouts of the residents or former residents. But then I had a stroke of good fortune. In the bottom drawer I discovered desk diaries covering a period of seven years, diaries which the police had overlooked during their short period of control over the premises. (I made several enquiries of police officers on this subject but failed to establish why this had occurred.) The handwriting inside was old-fashioned and I could discern that most of the entries were made by three different hands. I later tried unsuccessfully to determine beyond doubt whose handwriting was whose by sending letters to the three convicted Kincora staff, hoping for handwritten replies. Two replied in their own handwriting but McGrath requested the prison governor to reply on his behalf. All of them declined my request for an interview. But for now, all I saw were pages and pages of mundane information, recording everyday events in the life of Kincora, such as how much meat was to be delivered by the butcher and how much he was to be paid; the staff rota; the names of social services staff who telephoned about their clients. But there might be other material here worthy of investigation and I could not possibly note it all down in the time I had available inside the home. I had to 'borrow' the diaries.

Leaving Kincora with seven A-4 sized diaries tucked under my arm made me feel like a thief but I had a feeling that they would throw up leads which might provide new witnesses with more information about what had been going on inside the hostel. During the following forty-eight hours, two librarians at the BBC copied the diaries – every page in each diary for seven years, whether blank or not – in triplicate. I then returned the originals to the filing cabinet inside the hostel and set to work to make use of the diary entries. Many late nights were spent at home rifling the Xeroxed pages of the diaries for details of life in the hostel, noting names which were familiar to me because of the information I had already gathered or marking down intriguing minutiae which just might offer a new lead.

A number of references in the diary for 1975 related to a well known East Belfast City Councillor, Joshua 'Joss' Cardwell. He was a member of the City Council's Heath Committee and the committee's representative on the Personal Health and Social Services Committee of the Eastern Health Board; even so, the mentions of his name appeared rather unusual. For example, on Saturday 31 May: 'Visitation: Councillor Joss Cardwell, EHSSB.' Nothing unusual in a visit to check up on the wellbeing of the residents except that lower down on the same page it is noted: 'All residents on day outing to Groomsport and Bangor.' So if it was an official visit, why on a Saturday and why when, apparently, all the residents were on a day outing. There were many other references to 'visitations' by Cardwell, quite a few at weekends. It was time to visit Cardwell to see if he could provide any answers.

On two successive evenings I called at the Cardwell home, finding it in darkness. No one answered when I knocked, so on the third night I parked outside with a few bottles of Lucozade and a couple of newspapers and magazines, determined to await Cardwell's return. It was around 11 o'clock when his car drove up. He was making his way from the garage to the front door when I got to the gate and called out to him, explaining first of all who I was and the reason for my visit. His response was indistinct but I felt he was reluctant to tell me anything. I could see I was losing ground as he put the key in the front door. 'Mr Cardwell,' I called out from the pavement, 'can you tell me why you would visit Kincora when the boys were all away on a day out?' He stopped, glanced back in my direction and I knew that now I had his attention. He mumbled something about it being part of his duty to visit such homes because of his work on health committees and his duty to the boys in care. I rephrased the question. 'Were you always on official visits then?' He now showed signs of extreme discomfort. He stepped out of the doorway as if to come back towards me, stopping half-way across the narrow strip of garden. 'Did you have reason to visit Kincora other than as part of your duties?' He declined to answer and turned back towards the house. I kept pushing questions about the nature of his visits to the house. He kept mumbling and looking unsure about how to explain these visits, and for several minutes we exchanged words across his garden. At one stage he told me his visits to Kincora were none of my business and that he did not have to tell me about his private business. I agreed, but again asked why he would want to be in the home on days when the residents were not present. He eventually went inside, closing the door on this avenue of enquiry and leaving me standing on the pavement outside, pondering the reasons for his discomfort.

Had Cardwell faced up to the questions and offered some explanation for his irregular calls at Kincora, I might have been satisfied. But his whole demeanour left me suspicious about what was going on. Was he in some way involved in sexual activities with residents? Was he homosexual? Was he a pederast? What did he have to hide? Given that *The Irish Times* had opened the door on the whole Kincora court case in early 1982 by publishing a story about a 'homosexual vice ring' centred on the home and involving many prominent citizens, I was beginning to wonder if Cardwell had been mistreating young residents. Over the next few days, I wrestled with the dilemma of whether or not to get in touch with the police.

Eventually I resolved that if there was a likelihood that Cardwell had been sexually abusing young men at Kincora, I owed something to the boys who had already suffered so much and who had the courage to make statements to the police which were not just for their own benefit, but for that of future generations of children in care. I reported my concerns to the police. They interviewed Cardwell. A few days later he was found dead in his car, which was parked inside his garage. A pipe from the exhaust led into the car. It was a tragedy with which I have had to live ever since. A police officer not directly involved in the 1981 or 1982 police investigations, but who had been helpful to me on matters relating to the Kincora case, was extremely critical of my treatment of Cardwell. For many years I blamed myself, and it was only when one of the Kincora team of detectives spoke to me years later that my conscience was eased. He told me the police would have been interviewing Cardwell anyway because they had learned during their investigation that Cardwell was an active homosexual involved with the Town Solicitor, John A. Young, and Joseph Mains.

It is difficult to avoid the conclusion that Cardwell, with his personal knowledge of Mains, must have been aware of some of the complaints about Kincora going back over the years he served as Councillor. He must have seen Mains in homosexual activity with some of the more willing participants and as an elected representative his duty was certainly to the welfare of young men in care. Given that Mains was known to treat boys at Kincora by taking them out and about in his car, entertaining them at homosexual haunts in Belfast, it is very difficult to believe that Cardwell did not have suspicions.

My experience with Cardwell underlined my precarious position in these circumstances. As a reporter I had a duty to protect sources, to face imprisonment if necessary to protect a source, but as a citizen I have the same legal obligations as everyone else. I again decided to get in touch with the police when, some time later, I received an intriguing document which had been found inside Kincora. In all six pages were passed on to me by someone who at one time had had access to the office, and who had found them in a drawer in the desk. The person who supplied them asked not to be identified but thought they should be forwarded to the police.

These six pages offered advice on personal security, which in itself was not unusual given the times, but the wording of the advice is intriguing. It offers what could be regarded as the standard security advice issued to anyone in the security forces, business or politics about avoiding the same route, changing times of travel and hints on how to detect letter bombs. But there are one or two references which raise questions about the intended recipients of such a document. Firstly, on the page headed 'Security Away From Home,' the item listed as Number 13 says: 'Where there is advance publicity of your visit to areas which you consider sensitive you should contact your local police. Arrangements will then be made to give attention to your visit if necessary.' The term 'advance publicity' suggests this advice is aimed at those in the public eye. Three pages are marked Sections 'A', 'B', and 'C' although I cannot be sure now which of the three remaining pages goes with which section. However, on one of those three remaining pages under the heading 'Hotels', the following advice is offered: '1. If possible avoid use of the same hotel in any particular area. 2. When staying away from your residence never see visitors who are unknown or not vouchsafed in your suite; meet them in a public room where others will be present. This includes members of the press.' This indicates advice to some kind of VIP, perhaps a diplomat, possibly a politician – it is not your local beat bobby or army private.

Before officially handing these pages over to the police as requested by my source, I checked with a senior security officer. He thought that this document bore the hallmark of the Foreign Office. When handing it over and making a statement about how it came to be in my possession, I asked the officers who came to collect it if it could have been issued by the Foreign Office and one of them agreed it had that 'feel' about it. When I went back to the police they tried to tell me it had been issued to local businessmen, although there was a smile from the officer concerned. So I cannot be sure of the origins of the document. But if it is a Foreign Office document it offers a tantalising possibility. Its route to Kincora was through someone in contact with a person or persons who would have had need of advice on personal security from the Foreign Office ... and that leads us to McGrath.

Part IV
Guns and Politics 1974–80

9
McGrath, Tara, Guns and the Man from the Ministry

The summer of 1974 was a turning point in Adrian's life, when he realised the streets of London were not paved with gold. On 24 June he was sitting in an Irish bar when he spotted a copy of the Belfast *News Letter* lying on the counter, in a bundle of Irish papers. It was four days old but as he sipped his pint he flicked the pages for news of events back home and suddenly found himself engrossed in the full-page advertisement taken out by a loyalist group called Tara. He was immediately intrigued by the language; the phrase that really grabbed his attention was 'the hard core of Protestant resistance'. It had particular significance for him because a short time earlier he had lost a very close friend in Belfast, a victim of what he regarded as a sectarian assassination. He had not long returned to London from attending the funeral.

Adrian (not his real name) was just sixteen and had been brought up a Protestant, but not, he stresses, a bigot.

The advertisement advocated a new order in Ireland in which the Catholic Church would be abolished, yet for a loyalist grouping Tara seemed to be making some kind of attempt to understand what was happening politically and to have a willingness to try to deal with the problem without resorting to the tactics of other loyalist paramilitaries. 'As far as I was concerned,' he told me, 'there was more to loyalism than simply killing Catholics.' He responded to the PO box number provided and in due course received a reply from McGrath inviting him to a meeting in Belfast.

As Adrian prepared to travel to Belfast, his heart set on membership of Tara, he was unaware that by this stage Tara was increasingly attracting attention from elements of the security force intelligence network unfamiliar with McGrath's role in an MI5 operation to spy on the loyalist community. This operation was more crucial than ever given the successful UWC strike earlier that year which had brought down the power-sharing executive. Indeed, it seems as if McGrath's reputation as a homosexual held a fascination for members of Army Intelligence as early as 1973. In that year an English journalist, Kevin Dowling, then with the *Sunday Mirror*, was given a briefing by Colin Wallace, an Information Officer for the army at its Lisburn headquarters in Northern Ireland. Dowling confirmed this to me in 1982, recalling that Wallace described Tara as a 'bizarre homosexual army'. That generalisation, as we know, was well off the mark. In a further inaccuracy, the document named Roy Garland as McGrath's second-in-command, although since 1971 Garland had broken all links with McGrath and Tara.

It seems clear that the only reason Wallace and his

organisation had any information about McGrath was because by now the word was beginning to spread about his homosexuality, firstly from Dave in 1968 and from the intelligence unit of the Ulster Defence Regiment he had since joined. And secondly, of course, from Garland, who immediately informed the UVF members in Tara about McGrath. This was a difficult time for Garland, as his revelation resulted in a written death threat from, he believed, someone in Tara. The UVF members withdrew *en masse*, just as they had arrived, and according to Gusty Spence, they took with them, on his orders, as much of the Tara stockpile of weapons as they could lay their hands on. This did not mean the end of McGrath's gun-running. In the mid-1970s he was still able to gather around him a group of young men who shared his vision of the threat to Protestantism and to Ulster.

At about the same time Adrian was preparing for membership of Tara, two other recruits were being signed up. One was Charles Simpson; the other I cannot name for legal reasons but from this point on he will be referred to as Billy. The estimated total membership was between three and four hundred people, although by then it may have been considerably lower than the peak figure of 1969-70.

Adrian made his way up the Newtownards Road to McGrath's home for his first encounter with McGrath. He knocked on McGrath's front door and waited. The man answering certainly did not look like the archetypal loyalist paramilitary leader, with his cardigan, receding hair and glasses. McGrath beckoned his young guest indoors. Adrian recalls that the Tara OC came across as a gentle soul and the decor of the house, he says, was very Irish. 'It had a bohemian feel about it with lots of wood and rugs,' he told me. Mrs McGrath served tea and biscuits and Adrian discussed political developments in Northern Ireland and the destiny of the Protestant majority. This was a house and a routine he was to get to know very well over the years he remained in the organisation. As he left, Adrian told McGrath he would be staying with a relative and McGrath said that someone would be in touch.

Within a few days Ian Dawson called to see Adrian and for the next three years they became almost inseparable as they worked feverishly at preparations for the 'doomsday' McGrath assured them lay ahead. Adrian confesses that for a time he became 'almost addicted' to the afternoon discussion sessions in McGrath's front room. Adrian described the ruthlessness of McGrath's 'doomsday' plan to me:

> Sympathetic police officers and senior members of the British Army and Ulster Defence Regiment were already aware of Tara's plans. And a feature of the 'doomsday' plan was a night of the long knives. In the event of activating the plan Tara had briefed units to go to the homes of every loyalist paramilitary leader and the key figures in the unionist parties. Those not prepared to go along with the plan would simply be assassinated.

While Tara was of increasing interest in the world of the intelligence gatherers it seemed to be regarded by the police and others as a grouping with little direction and few teeth. With the guns of the IRA blazing on one side and those of the UVF and UDA on the other, Tara appeared to be all talk and no action. Certainly, when Adrian joined in 1974, the RUC had bigger fish to fry.

1974 began with the message from the Provisionals that they looked forward 'with confidence' to a year in which British rule in Ireland would be destroyed; the UDA response was to point out that the 'traditional unionist is dead ... loyalists now have to shape their own future.' Amid growing political squabbles in unionist circles, the former DUP chairman Desmond Boal was reported as saying he would now consider a federal Irish parliament together with a provincial Ulster parliament – a view quickly condemned by Paisley and Bill Craig but welcomed by Ruairi Ó Bradaigh, the Sinn Féin president, who said it was approximately what Sinn Féin had been proposing. The UVF praised Boal's 'courage and honesty' while Paisley told a radio audience that he was convinced Britain no longer wanted Northern Ireland.

Because Tara was not active, it was low on the list of security force priorities. However, McGrath secretly organised for a small group of members to be given weapons' training in a field outside Larne under the direction of Alan Gingles. This was concealed from the wider membership. Tara was run on a 'need-to-know' basis so it was not uncommon to find in discussions with former members that they were unaware of activities of others within the organisation. According to Clifford Smyth, this was a deliberate policy, devised by McGrath from the outset to protect the structure and activities of the organisation.

In 1974 McGrath secretly organised the importation of guns from abroad, an operation that was also subject to the need-to-know imperative. It appears that the shipment got caught up in the UWC strike and was trapped inside the blockaded port of Larne. At the conclusion of the strike, McGrath took delivery of a consignment of weapons from Holland, where his Protestant evangelical contacts had found sympathetic sources. The Dutch had provided Heckler and Kock rifles, American sub-machine guns and M-1 Carbine rifles, heavy German Spandeau machine guns and an assortment of ammunition.

McGrath's handlers in MI5 must have been aware of these activities but they took action to prevent any police investigation of McGrath, as I discovered when I met James, a former Army Intelligence officer who came to Northern Ireland late in 1974. James (not his real name) remembers that as soon as he arrived he began reading reports which were coming in about a group known as Tara. He tells an eye-opening story of how MI5 blocked his attempts to investigate and report to the police the activities of McGrath in Kincora. (The new recruits, Billy, Adrian and Simpson knew nothing of McGrath's sexuality at this stage and like the other members of Ireland's Heritage Lodge and Tara they were continuing with their efforts to be ready for 'doomsday'.)

McGrath busied himself with briefings on British security policy, quoting intelligence contacts he had, but never naming them. In this way he briefed Tara members about the IRA's strategy and the strategy of the Dublin government towards Northern Ireland, generally giving the impression that he was very well informed. On one occasion, according to Simpson and Billy, McGrath produced what looked like genuine Irish Army Intelligence documents at a meeting. Billy remembered seeing photographs of various houses of alleged IRA suspects as well as references to the Irish army's G-2 intelligence section. Whatever the source of these documents, McGrath certainly represented them as Irish Army Intelligence reports, giving the current assessment of IRA strengths and identifying factors that would necessitate Irish army action across the border in Northern Ireland. Certainly, Garland believed McGrath had contacts at government level in the Republic. McGrath travelled to the Republic, according to Billy, to set up Tara groups in Cavan, Monaghan and Donegal, with a brief to observe movements of Irish army and gardai along the border. Adrian also recalls such briefings. None of the three new recruits were in any doubt about the strategy for the 'doomsday' scenario: law and order would have completely broken down, the Army and RUC either disarmed or withdrawn to barracks prior to a total British withdrawal. McGrath's plan was that at this stage Tara would step in and provide leadership for the Protestant people, taking control of the rogue elements of the loyalist paramilitaries. A discussion took place at McGrath's home one afternoon with a 'stranger' present. The year was 1977, an eventful year for Adrian.

Early in the year, according to Adrian, McGrath had asked him if he wished to go on a short holiday, to get away for a few weeks. Adrian first thought he meant some kind of training camp but the Tara OC did not elaborate. He told Adrian that another member would get in touch with him.

The plan was for the two young men to travel out of Ireland through Dublin Airport to Brussels, then make their way to Holland by coach and train. Adrian likened the whole trip to something from a spy novel. On the trip he discovered from his travelling companion that there was good reason for the caution and the complicated itinerary. His companion had been to Holland six or seven months earlier to set up an arms deal but things had gone badly wrong. 'He told me he was with a man called Keck,' Adrian said, 'and they had gone to a back room of a bar to negotiate the deal when two men with guns burst in. As they made a run for it, the gunmen opened fire, hitting Keck in the leg. They both escaped and even found a doctor to treat Keck without reference to a hospital.' When they arrived at the small Dutch town Adrian and his companion were met by a man who drove them to a large house in a plush suburb. Adrian was amazed. 'Packed into the house and the garage was the most enormous arsenal of weapons I had ever seen,' he said. 'There were rifles, pistols, sub-machine guns and larger weapons, including an early German version of the M-60, I think it was called a Tornado. There were Mausers, Italian Berettas and thousands upon thousands of rounds of ammunition of all sorts.' On the first of several overnights at the house, Adrian was provided with a loaded pistol with instructions to keep it by his bed and orders not to open fire if intruders turned out to be Dutch police. The emphasis on long arms in this consignment was part of Tara policy: recognition that in a 'doomsday' situation rifles and the like would be of greater value militarily. Indeed, Adrian told me there had been trades in the past with other loyalist paramilitary groups like the UVF in which Tara members had exchanged as many as three handguns for a rifle.

The Tara duo made one other stop on the way to Amsterdam for the return journey, then left Holland hidden on the ship of a 'friendly skipper', and eventually re-entered Ireland through Dublin.

A few days after getting back, Adrian was urgently summoned to McGrath's home for an afternoon meeting. He was – as usual – ushered inside by McGrath himself, but once in the living room he realised this was not the normal session he had been accustomed to because there was a stranger sitting there. 'He was an elderly man,' Adrian told me, 'with long grey hair and wearing a pinstripe suit. McGrath introduced me to the stranger by name but did not give the visitor's name.' McGrath told Adrian that the guest had been very keen to meet him and for the next ninety minutes or so the three discussed the Northern Ireland situation in some detail. 'The stranger spoke with a very refined English accent,' said Adrian. 'I was in awe because I realised I was in the presence of someone very special, intellectually speaking. I was so in awe that I did not really make many contributions to the conversation.' Most of the debate was on the subject of the future of Northern Ireland inside the European community. 'McGrath and the Englishman felt that the EEC would eventually mean that the border between Northern Ireland and the Republic would become obsolete and there would, *de facto*, be a United Ireland.' Some kind of European peace-keeping force might then be the signal for Tara's units to put the 'doomsday' plan into action.

It was to be a few days before the full significance of the meeting with the stranger became clear to Adrian, and the clarification came from his companion on the Dutch trip. 'He asked me about the meeting,' said Adrian, 'so I told him about the stranger, the nature of the discussion he and McGrath had and I gave him my impressions of the stranger. I told him he seemed to have an impressive grasp of our situation and an admirable ability to speak about it. It was then that my companion stunned me. He told me the man I had met in McGrath's house was a senior Northern Ireland Office official at Stormont, someone with power and influence and who was a good friend of Tara's who would always be available to us!'

This man may well have been a senior British Intelligence official, a top MI5 officer, one of the politicial advisers who headed up MI5's operations in Northern Ireland. In McGrath's house? One of the two people who can truthfully answer the question of what an under-secretary was doing in McGrath's house is now dead and I have no means of knowing the identity, nor therefore the fate of the other, the man Adrian met that day. Could he have been a member of the Belfast–London committee? Clifford Smyth remembers that the Belfast–London committee was represented by McGrath as a caucus of people strongly supportive of the loyalist position in Northern Ireland

By the time Adrian met the under-secretary in 1977, McGrath had already taken the first steps to establishing yet another possible source of weapons and training, this time casting his eyes as far afield as Africa – once again with the apparent approval and even perhaps the assistance of those in MI5 who were responsible for controlling the loyalist operation.

10
OUT OF AFRICA

The people of Protestant Ulster traditionally had an affinity with white South Africa. They shared the seige mentality, the sense of living constantly under threat from neighbours who would not accept the political system and who resorted to violence as a means of expressing opposition to government policy. Many emigrants from Northern Ireland made new lives in 'white' African states such as Rhodesia and South Africa. In the case of the latter, another reason for affinity is the Afrikaners' Dutch Reformed Church. William McGrath engaged in correspondence with the white Prime Minister of Rhodesia, Ian Smith, often writing about the plight of the whites living there at a time when the black population was rebelling and seeking rights denied them by the ruling classes. On Friday 24 September 1976, McGrath raised the issue of Rhodesia at a lodge meeting, quoting Prime Minister Ian Smith's perception of an 'evil plan being worked out in front of our very eyes'. McGrath told his fellow brethren that he regarded Rhodesia 'as one of the last bastions of Christianity in that large continent'.

In 1976, the debate in unionist circles was dominated by the issue of direct rule from Westminster and McGrath's contribution was the publication of a Tara News Bulletin headlined: 'In Defence of Direct Rule!' On Tara's behalf he had written to all the former Convention members warning that plans for a United Unionist Action Council with the purpose of disrupting direct rule would not enjoy

Tara support. As the bulletin stated:

> Within the confines of clearly stated principles we have at all times sought to co-operate with others committed to defence of the Union and preservation of that way of life cherished by the majority of our people. On many issues, and particularly in respect of their proposals for future devolved government, we have supported our political leaders in their attempts to end uncertainty and instability in Northern Ireland. We well understand and identify with the feeling of our people for devolved government at Stormont. However, principally concerned with the Union, we must record our alarm at the mode of thought now apparent amongst some sections of the Unionist leadership. As Ulster Unionists we completely reject the suggestion that continued government by the United Kingdom Parliament is in any way unacceptable; and we declare our resolve to oppose any attempt to render continued Direct Rule unworkable.

Here we have a man linked to MI5 disseminating a message which is clearly aimed at discouraging unionists from confrontation with the Westminster government in an effort to re-establish power at Stormont: 'Traps have been set and plans devised by which it is hoped we will confront Parliament; and will ourselves set in motion a chain of events which will lead ultimately to the severing of the British link.' This bulletin is a clear indication that while McGrath had great sympathy for the plight of white

Rhodesians, he would support only full integration with Westminster and parity for Northern Ireland citizens as part of the United Kingdom.

According to Adrian and Billy, McGrath's contacts with Rhodesia did not stop at a sympathetic exchange of views with the Prime Minister. Both relate that in early 1976 McGrath sent a Tara member to Africa and, as Billy recalled, there were very specific instructions:

> I mentioned to you earlier that with the benefit of hindsight I believe Tara was essentially set up, funded and indeed organised by the British intelligence services, MI5 in particular, and when this person was sent to Rhodesia he was being sent to make contact with the intelligence community there. I can only conclude that McGrath had these connections because they were brought about by his very good connection with the British security services.

Adrian said the individual sent to Rhodesia did not make contact with McGrath for many months. It was as if 'he had disappeared off the face of the earth and McGrath was outraged by his lack of contact'. With one member 'missing' on the African continent, McGrath sent a second to Rhodesia – Charles Simpson. His mission was to gain valuable training which could be put to good use when he returned – training in counter-insurgency methods and intelligence-gathering techniques, with an emphasis on training for action behind enemy lines. Simpson says McGrath wanted him to join the Rhodesian Army's Armoured Car Regiment because they used the South African version of the Panhard armoured car – the gland type, according to McGrath, used by the Éire army. The intention was to have people who could properly use any such vehicles captured during conflict. There was little opportunity for members of Tara to gain military training – except for the few involved in the local security forces – and clearly McGrath regarded Rhodesia and the conflict there as an opportunity not only for training, but perhaps also as a means of identifying possible routes for the acquisition of weapons from friendly sources.

The first Tara member sent to Africa eventually briefly returned to Northern Ireland, making the trip to Holland with Adrian in 1977, before he returned to Rhodesia to join up with Simpson in the Rhodesian Army. Simpson returned to Northern Ireland in late 1979 or early 1980, applying to rejoin the Ireland's Heritage Lodge in May 1980 before going on to South Africa, where he joined the South African Police. Gingles had also moved to South Africa in 1980, after Rhodesia became Zimbabwe. He served with the South African Defence Force as a member of 5 Recce Commando based at Phalaborwa. This unit was inherited by South Africa from one set up by the Rhodesian Central Intelligence Organisation during the war there. Under the South Africans, it was used as a support group for Renamo, a guerrilla army operated by the South Africans on the Mozambique border. In October 1981, Gingles died while placing explosives on a vital railway line inside Mozambique. This the South Africans wanted to sabotage in order to damage Mozambique's export trade which used the link between Malawi and the port of Beira. The name of Lieutenant Alan Gingles appears on the South

African war memorial at Fort Klapperkop in Pretoria.

According to Billy, McGrath also had contacts within the South African intelligence services, and soon a third member of Tara would move to South Africa. In July 1980, Billy travelled to London with McGrath and was astounded when McGrath took him to the South African Embassy for a meeting with two senior officials, one of whom was directly linked with military intelligence, the other with BOSS. He recalls that the conversation centred on the links between the IRA, SWAPO (the South West African People's Organisation) and the ANC. The officials had a list of weapons allegedly supplied by SWAPO to the IRA and stated that some had been found in an IRA cache in Coagh, County Tyrone. These weapons had originated, it was claimed, in Eastern Germany, and this, according to the South Africans, proved the communist connections with terrorist organisations. Because of the IRA connections with subversives in their country the South Africans allegedly told McGrath that they could give a commitment from their government to the cause of Northern Ireland's loyalists. Billy says that no definite arrangement was made at this meeting but McGrath had been asked to think about how the South Africans could be of assistance. (At this time McGrath was already under investigation by police for sexual abuses at Kincora, so it would seem there was no chance of his being in a position to follow up this contact with the South Africans.)

As a result of this meeting Billy was persuaded to go to South Africa, his passage eased and assured by the two men he met in London. He admired the white South Africans, particularly the Afrikaners, especially so, he told me, after the meeting in the South African Embassy. He could see clear parallels with the situation of his own people in Northern Ireland, a common struggle against communism, against rampant black or Irish nationalism. 'We have,' he told me, 'the same work ethic as the Afrikaners.' Soon Billy was working for the South African Defence Forces, at around the same time as Simpson and Gingles. Through other Northern Ireland contacts, unrelated to McGrath or Tara, Billy had eventually become involved with the security branch of the South African police and it was to involve him in one bizarre intelligence operation centred on a British agent who also happened to be a very senior figure within the UDA

In July 1985 Billy was working in the Eastern Transvaal on an internal security project when he was summoned to Pretoria for a meeting with a senior officer. There was a problem with an operation being run by another unit of South African military intelligence which involved an Irish connection and Billy was tasked to help them to resolve the difficulty. He was briefed on the situation: a man from Northern Ireland had arrived in South Africa to make a deal for arms for loyalist paramilitaries. His name was Brian Nelson, and he was at the time intelligence coordinator for the UDA. Contacts had met him and taken him to his hotel and there had been a few preliminary meetings, but now they wanted Billy to meet Nelson to determine how genuine he was, to discover as much as possible about the man and to report back to them for further instructions before making the necessary introductions. Billy was provided with details of Nelson's time of arrival, the location where he could make contact with him and very little else. But then, in what Billy describes as a 'bizarre turn of events', he was told on the morning of his proposed meeting with Nelson that his part in the operation had been called off. It appears that a direct contact in Belfast had warned that Nelson could not be trusted as there was a suspicion he was an agent for the British.

The communication from Belfast sparked off a day of frantic meetings in South Africa, especially in Durban, where Nelson was to be based during his visit. Late in the day Billy's operation got the go-ahead and he was dispatched to meet the UDA man at the unimpressive Plaza Hotel in Broad Street near the marketplace. Billy was not impressed by Nelson, describing him as someone who did not have the air of authority which goes with a worldly-wise traveller and indeed, the first thing Nelson told Billy was that he had been mugged by a group of blacks earlier that day. Billy left Nelson in his hotel that night after making an arrangement to meet next day.

When Billy reported back, his controller told him that the 'mugging' was the work of black undercover members of the security police, organised because there was a belief that Nelson was taping meetings with contacts. The undercover men had indeed found tapes, although they did not invite Billy to listen to them. Nelson's wallet and diary had also been taken. The brigadier in charge of the Durban operation told Billy that Nelson had been under tight surveillance from the moment he arrived and instructed Billy to be ready for another session with Nelson next day to get more information. The following day Nelson was taken to a gun shop which was a front for Armscor and was introduced to the man who ran the shop. Eventually he was taken to a secret store underground and shown a selection of weapons. Later Billy spent time with Nelson, trying to glean as much information as possible about his background without raising suspicions. Nelson told Billy that he was in the UDA, that he had been a British soldier and had at one time driven a truck in Germany. He claimed he spoke German fluently although, according to Billy, he appeared to have forgotten the language when Billy tried a few sentences. Before leaving Nelson that night, Billy handed him a sealed envelope – Billy thought it contained money in English notes – to pass on to someone back in Belfast. Billy said his farewells and never saw Nelson again.

A few days after Nelson's departure Billy was called in by the brigadier and informed that Nelson had been followed all the way back to Belfast by South African Intelligence. At Heathrow Airport, he was watched leaving the airport and travelling the short distance to the Heathrow Park Hotel where he met two men. He was observed showing the men photographs he had been given in South Africa of various weapons Armscor proposed to give to the UDA. It was clear that Nelson was a British agent, deliberately placed within the UDA many years before by military intelligence and MI5. Billy says that as a result of their surveillance on Nelson, the South Africans severed all links with the UDA and closed this operation to supply weapons. No weapons were dispatched on this occasion although some years later a large shipment was sent to Northern Ireland – but only because it was arranged by someone outside the UDA, someone in Ulster Resistance who had good contacts in South Africa. Although not directly involved on this occasion, Nelson was still in a position to keep British Intelligence informed of every development and no attempt was made to intercept the whole consignment although, funnily enough, the UDA share of the spoils was intercepted by the police outside Portadown. The other two-thirds of the shipment was divided between Ulster Resistance and the UVF. Many of those weapons are still in circulation, although some were recovered by the police. How much involvement McGrath's former Tara members had in the procurement of this shipment is not known. Simpson's name has been mentioned as a key player in this operation but he has denied it to me. Billy, surprisingly, simply refuses to talk about it.

McGrath's conviction and imprisonment, which happened during 1980 and 1981, rule him out of the frame for the Ulster Resistance consignment of weapons. But British Intelligence were prepared to use another of their agents, Nelson, to keep open the South African arms supply line. What started with McGrath's soundings in the mid to late 1970s and even with his visit to London in early 1980 when he was already under investigation, was concluded with the successful shipment in 1989. Under the guiding hand of MI5, some Tara members were encouraged to go to Rhodesia and on to South Africa, exchanging information about IRA activities in Northern Ireland and identifying their links with the military wing of the ANC, *Umkhonto wie Siswe*, (known as MK). Ultimately the South African government adopted a policy of tacit support to loyalists, following up with arms supplies. They were encouraged to do so by loyalists who could provide the sanction-ridden South African state with much needed missile technology stolen by sympathisers from Shorts in Belfast. In short, the intention of British Intelligence, through McGrath and Tara, and then through Nelson of the UDA, was to maintain some kind of control over loyalist violence to counter that of the IRA. Given this desire to have control of what can only be viewed as pro-state terrorism, it is small wonder MI5 were so keen to block the 1982 police investigation by the RUC and Sir George Terry. It also explains why MI5 stopped Army Intelligence from their investigation of McGrath and Tara. There is, of course, one other fascinating possibility which would put a very different complexion on the whole business: that McGrath and Nelson knew each other.

11
Shadow Politics

Army Intelligence officer James had just been posted to Northern Ireland. From a Christian family, he had with him a list of a number of Christian families known to his parents from previous visits, families he might get in touch with when he had time to socialise. But he was soon to have cause to meet them on business. In the files he inherited, he read a report about a Protestant evangelical paramilitary leader, William McGrath, OC of Tara. Then an incoming report about Tara caught his eye.

James cannot be absolutely certain but he believes his interest was stimulated by a report of three or four pages – which included biographies of the leading members – stating that some members of Tara were using an Orange lodge as a cover for weapon training and drill nights. In the professional circles in which James was mixing socially at the time no one could answer his questions about this strange group called Tara, but he also noticed references to the homosexual leader of the group which stated that he was involved in evangelical Christian activities. He moved out into the Christian community where he and his family had contacts and got permission to seek information from within Tara. There was one particular source he wished to tap, someone with a background similar to his own, a member of Tara, referred to hereafter as Sidney. James telephoned him, introduced himself as a Christian and the two men arranged to meet. James skirted around the subject of Tara, but, crucially, he was finding out first-hand just how knowledgeable Sidney was on political affairs. James was impressed by his grasp of the situation and with his ability to analyse paramilitary thinking on both sides of the religious divide. Eventually James and Sidney became good friends and there was never any mention of James's work, although he believed Sidney knew what was going on. James noticed that Sidney never mentioned Tara or his involvement in it and spoke only once in general terms of William McGrath, as an associate in the Orange Order.

Then Sidney asked James a question that shook him. He wondered if his friend McGrath could be working for MI5, as apparently McGrath had told Sidney that he did. James says he believed that this was a figment of McGrath's imagination, particularly as he had already been told about McGrath's sexual activities. This MI5 business might just be a fantasy life invented by McGrath to use with people he might want to seduce. In any event, James began to feed the information he was getting from Sidney into the military intelligence system and soon he found himself travelling to Army Headquarters in Lisburn where he reported directly to the political adviser of the Intelligence Section, HQNI, someone who was not an army officer and described by James as a civil servant, but who nevertheless participated in everything that was going on in the Intelligence Section. This man's main interest, according to James, was intelligence of a political nature on the Protestant side. He seemed pleased with the information gathered by James and a good working relationship developed between the two, with the political adviser encouraging James to continue in the hope he would get even better quality intelligence.

In the spring of 1975 there was an even greater need for good quality intelligence on all activities in the unionist community, political and paramilitary, because of the success of the UWC strike the previous year. Increasingly, loyalist paramilitaries were flexing their muscles. James was slowly building up an improved picture of McGrath and Tara when he got another breakthrough. From his earlier general enquiries in evangelical Christian circles came a response from someone who knew someone who had information about Tara, from the inside. So it was that James visited the home of a retired vet seven miles south of Belfast in Carryduff. His host, to use James's own words, 'tapped on my heart to find out if Jesus Christ was inside, putting his fingers on my spiritual pulse.' Once satisfied that he was talking to a Christian, Jim McCormick agreed to help James to set up a meeting with a former member of Tara. He told him about another Christian who was attempting, with little success, to get the RUC to investigate McGrath, someone by the name of Roy Garland. McCormick duly set up the meeting with Garland.

When McCormick mentioned Garland's name, James remembered seeing it on the Tara file with a question mark as to whether he was still an active member. In fact Garland had broken off all links with McGrath and Tara in 1971 and had spent most of the intervening years trying to get the police and a number of politicians to take action to bring about a serious investigation of William McGrath. James found Garland sincere and his story horrendous. According to James, Garland explained that Tara was an organisation of men who 'rather fancy themselves as a provisional government for the day when all things collapse'. This, he said, was the 'doomsday' plan. More important from James's point of view was the information from Garland that McGrath exerted an influence over young men involved in religious activities and that there were sexual overtones to the whole business. 'I began to wonder what on earth we were getting into when Garland began to accuse McGrath of a selection of sexual perversions,' said James. 'The gist of the thing is that McGrath found out the little sexual weaknesses the various individuals had and then began to play on them. He also told me McGrath was a homosexual.'

Garland told James that McGrath worked in Kincora, a hostel for teenage boys, and James seems to remember that there was some mention of this on the file he had viewed back at the office. Garland said he was concerned that McGrath was working in the hostel, concerned about the boys resident there. 'I believed Garland,' James said. 'He was telling the truth. It obviously had to be investigated, I was certainly looking to ask other people questions.' But first James has to write up a report and a further meeting was arranged with Garland. James was not able to attend this meeting although he was made aware of what was discussed. The second meeting was held at James's offices.

James and his colleagues who interviewed Garland the second time studied the new information Garland had provided and compared it with the notes in the file before compiling a report to feed into the military system. What happened then? James explained:

> At this stage this matter is not connected with the

> political adviser. We would write the information down, circulate it to the places that we thought it should be circulated and then await, you know... future response, what comes next. In many ways, the ball bounces backwards and forwards from one side of the court to the other and in Intelligence matters very rarely are you actually in control of the ball. Often you are receiving what you can get.

On this occasion James fed the information upwards. 'This was not an investigation which had daily pursuit,' he said. 'It was an investigation that was riding along with other enquiries... in my case more into Protestant affairs but not exclusively so. There was a lot of intelligence activity; that was one small thread in a large fabric.'

It may have been a small thread, but it certainly got the attention of the political adviser because eventually James was invited to the Lisburn headquarters to see him. The message was passed on to James by his immediate superior. 'I was expecting tasking for my other Tara contact,' James said. 'Bear in mind information has gone in on Tara and we have got a link. I cannot honestly say that I was expecting to receive gold stars but I went up feeling pretty positive, expecting a normal meeting.' This is what happened when he met the man in charge of the Intelligence Section at Lisburn Army headquarters:

> I got blown out of his office. He was rude to me. He told me that the kind of information that I submitted was not proper intelligence, that we had nothing, we as intelligence officers did not dabble

in homosexual affairs, that these moral matters were nothing to do with us. He vilified my report, he told me no more meetings with Garland, to drop the investigation into Tara and also he told me to cut off the contact (with Sidney). I can remember him saying to me, words to the effect, 'Get rid of him... break the contact, just get rid.' I was surprised because we had had a pretty good relationship until then. He blew me out of the office.

James was not in a position to question the political adviser's judgement but he tried to point out that he was doing only what he thought best, fighting back as best he could under the circumstances. He admitted that 'the wind was out of my sails'. He continued:

I certainly did not accept the moral protestations. Until then, everything that I had come across in terms of morality in intelligence circles was largely founded on the end justifies the means. I had never heard anyone speak about what is right and what is wrong. I was confused. He (the political adviser) was aggressive. He stood up, poo-pooing me... making me feel like a small boy, a wee small boy. So I was shocked. I had not come across this before in any other of the more senior intelligence officers or in him.

Perhaps this intelligence officer reacted the way he did because James was presenting a rather far-fetched story for which he had no actual evidence, only allegations, gossip and a bit of rumour. James could justify his position:

> The only way you can start to find out what real intelligence is, is to start with gossip and rumour and then try to get the information that corroborates it, and I was surprised and furthermore it ran parallel with other information that was coming in about Tara because the order of battle we had was confirmed by Garland, McGrath's position in it and the other names that were listed. Furthermore, this was an organisation that was ostensibly political, this was why I believed the political adviser was interested in it in the first place. So I was taken aback. As I walked away, my first reaction was, well maybe he is right. Has it been just a bit of Walter Mitty fantasy? Have we gone into a cul-de-sac here? But subsequent events have obviously proved... history shows that it was not the case.

James did not obey the order to cut off all contact with Sidney, although he did go some way towards doing what the political adviser had instructed him to do: he no longer pursued Sidney. James let Sidney go on making contact with him simply making excuses about why he could not meet. Until the day Sidney called with what he described as some 'very important information'. James wanted a meeting, but he was under orders not to, and as a soldier he had to seek permission before he could go ahead.

'I went back that morning and obtained permission to recontact the source,' James said. 'I went to my direct boss although I suspect he went to the political adviser.' With approval from his authorities, James set off to a Belfast cemetery for the meeting and what he learned there was to make him the political adviser's 'blue-eyed boy.' Sidney informed James that certain political figures were seriously examining the possibility of UDI and in the short term were planning an annoucement to that effect. It was now 1976, and the political adviser was delighted at the intelligence gathered by James from the same source with which he was told to break contact the previous year. As James recalled:

> He said this looks like he (Sidney) could become a very good source and should be cultivated ... money is no object ... would you like to make more meetings. I came away happy but again something in my mind was saying what is going on? And even more so after I have had another meeting with some of this gentleman's colleagues and it is obvious that their view about homosexuality and his [the political adviser's] view about the morality of homosexuality are widely divergent.

James then recounted a meeting with MI5 in London. ('They were not wearing their MI5 T-shirts,' James said, 'but ... ') at which he discussed a number of items he saw on a briefing note. Kincora was not the most relevant, but what did emerge was their interest in a man called John McKeague, a known homosexual in East Belfast. Let James describe the discussion:

> These gentlemen did not appear to be as well briefed as I was, particularly on McKeague. According to them they had some compromising film of a

homosexual nature of John McKeague and they wondered could this be used to make McKeague cooperative as an informant.

Aside from the discrepancy in moral attitude between these MI5 officers in London and the political adviser in Lisburn, the question of using McKeague's homosexuality as a lever to push him into providing information was a really strange development. I have spoken to another former Army Intelligence officer (Dennis from this point) at present domiciled in Northern Ireland who recalls that when he came here in 1975, one of his tasks was to take over running McKeague who had, apparently, previous dealings with a different Army Intelligence agent. Dennis had another interesting tale to tell.

When Dennis reported to Castlereagh Barracks in East Belfast in November 1975 for his second tour of duty in Army Intelligence, he was given a briefing by the officer he was succeeding. They went through the files, pausing at one on a loyalist group known as Tara. The outgoing officer informed Dennis that he had collected some intelligence on this organisation and filed it away because he could not find an existing file to place the information ... at least nothing in his own office. His departing colleague warned Dennis that if he knew what was good for him he should not do any digging on Tara. However, Dennis did dig around and when he had sufficient material he prepared a report which was sent up the chain of command. This produced a rocket from above, telling him in no uncertain terms to drop his enquiries, and he realised he had touched on a 'hot potato.' He had no authorisation to look at Tara and he believed from the nature of the rebuff that his report had gone from brigade level all the way up to Lisburn. As far as he could recall, the report mentioned McGrath being a homosexual but did not mention Kincora. He never again looked at the file.

At the end of 1975 or early in 1976, Dennis was tasked by his boss to escort a civilian around Belfast. There was nothing unusual about this type of request; it happened quite often when visiting intelligence officers wanted to see around the city. There was no explanation or introduction by name. The stranger was simply taken to a car where Dennis and a colleague were to drive him wherever he wished to go, but unlike many others in this situation who depend of the drivers to show them around Belfast, this individual had his own ideas about where he wanted to be taken. Dennis said he spoke with an English accent and was dressed smartly in jacket, trousers and cravat. He directed them to a house in East Belfast and left the two men in the car as he went inside. It was not until the Kincora story broke in 1980 that Dennis realised the house where he had dropped the stranger was in fact Kincora.

In 1990, I made contact by telephone with the political adviser at his home in England. He simply referred me to the Northern Ireland Office.

Part V
The Beginning of the End
1980-82

12
Day 1: Thursday 24 January 1980

The staff at Kincora Working Boys' Hostel in East Belfast were going about their duties as normal on the morning of 24 January 1980 but they were soon to receive news that would abruptly end the routine and leave an indelible mark on all their lives, forever damning the three principal members of staff as sex offenders. Two of those three, Joseph Mains the hostel warden and his deputy Raymond Semple were attending to the morning routine. As neither Mains or Semple were readers of the Dublin newspaper, the *Irish Independent*, they were unaware of the breaking of a scandal which would soon engulf them, along with the third member of staff, house father William McGrath.

I know what was going on inside Kincora that morning because Raymond Semple told me. In 1990 I visited Semple at his home in the Shore Road area of Belfast. By this time he had served his five-year term in prison and had been quietly reabsorbed into society. At the age of sixty-nine, he lived alone in his terraced home with a large Alsatian dog for company, the same dog he threatened to turn on me during another visit some weeks later. During this first visit Semple spoke candidly about his clear memories of events at Kincora on that fateful day in 1980. According to Semple, he and Joe Mains were 'astonished' when they received what he described as a 'panic call from the Holywood Road offices of the Eastern Health and Social Services Board'. The managers from their head office ordered a meeting with all the staff before lunchtime. Mains and Semple were ordered to get in touch with everyone employed at the hostel – including those not on duty that day – to instruct them to attend the meeting. Semple says McGrath, who lived just a few doors away from the hostel on the Upper Newtownards Road, could not be informed in time for this meeting and was told to turn up later that afternoon.

Irish Independent reporter Peter McKenna spent months checking the story before submitting it for publication:

> A major scandal erupted in the North last night on allegations of an 'official cover-up' over the recruiting of boys at a Belfast children's home for homosexual prostitution. The matter is to be raised at Westminster by Independent MP Gerry Fitt, who was 'shocked to the core' by the reports. 'If these allegations are true, there has been some kind of Watergate cover-up and those responsible should be brought to book.' The shock allegations about the home on the outskirts of the city resulted in a police report being sent to the Director of Public

Prosecutions. But no action was taken – and reports on certain cases were destroyed under orders from a senior member of the Social Services Department, it is claimed. A member of the staff at the boys' home is alleged to be involved with a loyalist paramilitary group. Officials in the Health Department were told this, but he has retained his job despite being suspected of encouraging children to engage in homosexual acts for money, and accepting payments for pimping.

Had Mains and Semple read that day's *Irish Independent* they would have noticed that there was no mention by name of the Kincora Working Boys' Hostel on the Upper Newtownards Road, but it is interesting that everyone involved in social work knew immediately which establishment was being referred to. Health service mandarins were quick to recognise the subject of the story and there were also two police officers who, over breakfast, took more than a passing interest in the 'exclusive' report. After reading it in detail, one of them immediately gathered his thoughts, his files, and without prompting from anyone, reported at once to RUC headquarters at Knock in Belfast.

A newspaper story originating in Dublin set in motion a chain of reactions all over Belfast and beyond, not least at Stormont, the seat of power and government (even under direct rule) in Northern Ireland. The *Irish Independent* soon reached the desk of RUC Chief Inspector George Caskey, the officer chosen to lead the Kincora enquiry team.

As the police began to structure their investigation, life

for McGrath went on as normal. As secretary of Ireland's Heritage LOL 1303 he was required to attend the monthly lodge meeting the day following publication of the *Irish Independent* story. His demeanour at the lodge meeting in Clifton Street Orange Hall on Friday 25 January 1980 – a meeting chaired by his son Worthington, the Worshipful Master – betrayed neither anxiety nor remorse. After the minutes for the previous meeting had been read William McGrath informed the lodge that he: 'and other brethren connected with the Tara group were the object of a malicious and evil attack in the Dublin press'. This drew a remark of support from the lodge treasurer, Brother William Quee (a leading member of the UDA, who was murdered by the Irish People's Liberation Organisation on 7 September 1988 outside his confectionary shop in North Belfast). Brother Quee assured Brother McGrath that he had the 'full support of the lodge during this troubled time'. McGrath had been chosen as secretary of the Lodge at the regular monthly meeting held on 26 October 1979 but as 1980 got under way, he faced the future with uncertainty.

By the next meeting of the lodge, on Friday 29 February, McGrath would have been aware that a major police investigation was underway but he again protested his innocence, giving members of the lodge further information 'regarding the slander campaign being conducted by the Dublin press' and asking the brethren for their 'continued prayers'. It is interesting to note that by the time the March meeting of the lodge took place, on Friday 28 March, there was no mention in the official records of the problems facing the secretary – who by that time had been suspended from his duties at Kincora and who had good reason to remember the name Caskey.

13
CAGING THE BEAST

Chief Inspector George Caskey sat at his desk, a copy of the day's *Irish Independent* spread out before him, the two dusty police files laid out alongside. It was late, nearly midnight on 24 January 1980, and the Chief Inspector's thoughts were on the day's events which had unexpectedly brought him to an urgent meeting at RUC headquarters at Knock in East Belfast with Assistant Chief Constable William Meharg. He was briefed on the views of the Chief Constable Sir John Hermon and the other senior officers who had already studied the newspaper article. As Head of Crime, Assistant Chief Constable Meharg consulted with the chiefs of his department, experienced officers of the calibre of Chief Superintendent Bill Mooney and Superintendent Desmond Brown. After close study of the reports which had been brought to headquarters by Detective Constable Cullen and further deliberations, they reported back to the Chief Constable in person. Sir John directed them to begin an immediate investigation.

Some time between seven and eight that evening, Chief Inspector Caskey was instructed to clear his desk of all other enquiries and establish a team of officers to conduct an investigation into the allegations about Kincora. Once he had completed a preliminary investigation he was to report back as a matter of urgency. Chief Inspector Caskey was not going to be rushed into an ill-conceived investigation but made time to study all the available material. Besides, his first priority was to choose the team of detectives he wanted.

A highly respected investigator, George Caskey had cut his teeth during some of the most violent days in the history of Northern Ireland. By 1980 head of the Serious Crime Squad, he had witnessed eleven years of seemingly mindless violence which had left a scar on society and on the police officers themselves. The burden for solving the rapidly growing catalogue of murders fell on the Serious Crime Squad, the brainchild of the previous Chief Constable, Sir Kenneth Newman, prompted by a Scotland Yard enquiry two years earlier into the activities of Sinn Féin.

The Kincora enquiry would throw up very different challenges for Caskey and his team. Not only would they have to muster all their investigative skills to solve crimes going back more than two decades; they would have to do so in a very sensitive manner. Before he left for home that night, Chief Inspector Caskey, who was to be promoted to Superintendent before the conclusion of the investigation (and who has since been further promoted to Chief Superintendent), made the decision to spend a few days sifting through the small amount of information available before he made his first moves. Already names of detectives were passing through his mind but he would make no appointments for some days while he read and reread the scanty documentation available.

The first name pencilled in on his list was Sergeant Berkeley Elliott, the most senior collator in the RUC, a man trained by Scotland Yard who was by now passing on his skills through a force training programme. For his second-in-command he wrote down the name of former schoolteacher Ted Cooke, a Chief Inspector with sound academic qualifications and a sharp brain for organising and coordinating. There was Chief Inspector John Middlemiss, formerly of Scotland Yard, who was regarded as a strong, competent and meticulous investigator with an ability to get straight to the heart of any problem. Then there was Detective Inspector Jim McClure who, like George Caskey, went on to become a Chief Superintendent. Another highly respected member of a team which at one time was more than twenty strong was Detective Sergeant Austin Wilson, later promoted to the rank of Chief Inspector, but who was murdered by the IRA in the grounds of Magee College in Derry in March 1986. As faces began to fill places on George Caskey's team sheet, he gathered up his files and headed for home.

Over the next few days, George Caskey concentrated on establishing how and why the hostel functioned, examining in detail the legislation used to send to Kincora young men who had the misfortune to find themselves wards of court. Although a small number were placed there on a voluntary basis, most were sent under the Children and Young Persons Act (1968), subjects to what were known as 'fit persons orders'. This meant that the child or adolescent became the responsibility of the Social Services Department until the order was revoked by the court or the individual reached the age of eighteen. Caskey studied the position of Kincora within the Department of Health and Social Services and saw that the running of the hostel was the direct responsibility of the Eastern Health and Social Services Board. He noted that Mains and Semple had the 'sleeping in the hostel' duties and that they, as the warden and deputy warden, were answerable to the management staff of the Eastern Health Board's

Castlereagh office. District management had a statutory duty to visit residential homes at least once a month and to send reports of their visits to the Director of the Eastern Health Board. The Personal Social Services Committee of the Eastern Health Board, of which Unionist Councillor Josh Cardwell was a member, had a responsibility to visit residential homes quarterly, also reporting back to the Board.

Not surprisingly Caskey found it a challenge to understand the cumbersome management structures in the health and social services which dated from the reorganisation of local government in the mid-1970s. Once contact had been established with those responsible at the Eastern Health Board for the day-to-day running of residential homes like Kincora, the Board's assistant director Bob Bunting became the liaison with the police. Conversations with Bunting produced new intelligence for the police, which further strengthened their initial opinions that there was substance to the allegations of sexual impropriety. In the meantime, Caskey learned how the hostel was supposed to be run under the stipulated terms of reference given to staff there.

At the same time he studied the dusty police files presented to him at police headquarters the first day he was summoned there, one containing information about two previous police investigations into Kincora conducted by Detective Constable Jim Cullen. The other, which had been uncovered in the archives, had been compiled by a Detective Constable John Scully. Both files had been completed in the 1970s. Caskey read the newspaper article so often he knew he could recite it – his method of getting a feel for the full extent of the problem. He felt he had to establish contacts outside the home that would be above suspicion – individuals who would be able to give him direction through the complicated procedures about to be tackled. Because of the breadth of the allegations, Caskey decided that was not a case for moving in and taking a narrow view, in other words it was not an occasion for rushing into a confrontation with those against whom the allegations had been made.

After several days of study it was time for Caskey to call his team together. A glance at the Cullen and Scully files suggested there might be something at the hostel worthy of rigorous investigation. For example, the Cullen file made it clear to him that there was a homosexual working at Kincora by the name of William McGrath, while the Scully file detailed threats made by a resident at Kincora to police when he had been arrested for questioning about petty crime. The boy repeated to police that he wanted Joe Mains brought down to the station immediately and that if he did not come quickly he would have reason to regret it. At no stage did he tell police what he meant by this threat, although Detective Scully felt strongly enough about the boy's tone to make a point of reporting it personally to the appropriate director of social services. From the Scully report George Caskey got the name of a resident with whom to begin his investigation. As events unfolded, this young man was one of the first to be interviewed by police.

Before any of the interviews took place one other piece of archive material came to light in the Cullen file which intrigued Caskey. It was a reference to an anonymous call made to police on 23 May 1973. During Cullen's investigation in 1974 he interviewed Roy Garland, former second-in-command of Tara, who revealed to the police officer that it was he who had made the anonymous call. Caskey immediately identified this piece of material as a crucial factor. Garland was about to become a key player in unravelling the whole Kincora affair, for if what he had to say in the anonymous call was true, Caskey realised that this alone was a matter worthy of investigation.

In later years, Caskey would marvel at the accuracy of the comments made by Garland in 1973. Garland began by referring to a vice ring being operated at Kincora and centred around William McGrath who was, he said, employed there as 'a social worker'. McGrath was practising various kinds of homosexual perversions and active in underground politics and in unionist politics. Furthermore, Garland stated, McGrath was not adverse to pressurising boys in the Young Unionist movement into adopting his policies in accordance with his objectives. Garland claimed to the police that McGrath was in contact with politicians who were known for their homosexuality and that this had been the means of getting him (McGrath) a job in social work. The RUC file shows that in 1973 Garland also informed the police that McGrath was leader of a secret organisation known as Tara and had contacts in London and further afield, outside the British Isles. Boys in care at Kincora, he told them, were open to exploitation – sexually, politically and financially.

When Caskey finished studying this material in the Cullen file, he was ready to make his first moves in his 'rigorous investigation'. By the time he got his case into court Caskey remarked: 'We knew within three days of the investigation getting under way that there was substance to the allegations carried in the *Irish Independent*. As evidence of sexual malpractice was gathered, the most sordid case came to light. It involved William McGrath and his brutal rape of a boy in the most vile circumstances. It upset everyone involved in our team. It was sickening in the extreme.'

One of the first people naturally listed for interview was Peter McKenna, the *Irish Independent* reporter, but Caskey knew he needed to speak urgently to some of the residents of the hostel. He had the name of one young man from the Scully file but he needed others. So, having called in his team of detectives, Chief Inspector Caskey first ordered the seizure of the register at Kincora which contained the names of residents, past and present. This documentation was central to the police investigation as it supplied detectives with the names of one hundred and eighty-six invividuals who had lived in the hostel between 1963 and 1980. Over the next weeks and months the RUC traced one hundred and four of these young men. Thirty-three of them made statements alleging homosexual abuses at Kincora.

Before his team of officers began searching for those whose names appeared in the official register, Caskey gave them one final briefing to emphasise the need for great sensitivity when approaching individuals who had had the misfortune to have been resident at Kincora. Most had settled down to life outside the hostel, a number were married with children and were holding down jobs to support their families. Diplomacy was vital in any approach, so much so that officers in many instances had to invent reasons for knocking the door of a married man who might not have told anyone of his difficulties at Kincora, least of all his wife. One of the most common tactics used to disguise the true purpose of the call was to enquire about unpaid parking tickets.

Several weeks passed after Peter McKenna's story on the front page of the *Irish Independent*. Life at Kincora continued, with Mains, Semple and McGrath going about their duties and still collecting their wages. The RUC team was in no hurry for a confrontation with the three staff members and even though senior officers believed there was a *prima facie* case to be answered, they moved very circumspectly in the construction of the case. Virtually every member of the Serious Crime Squad, numbering around twenty at the time, was now involved in searching out the truth. By now the police team was in daily contact with Bob Bunting, the conduit for the provision of earlier files, some of which were found in dusty office basements.

The first of the former residents to be interviewed was the young man whose name was one of the two the police had to go on initially. They found him living with a relative in Lancashire in England and he was interviewed around 25 February. The big breakthrough came within the next week, on 3 March. George Caskey himself and Sergeant Elliott found the second young man in London. He turned out to be very voluble and made a statement alleging that McGrath had sexual relations with him while he was living at Kincora. This was the beginning of the end for the three Kincora staff members. Caskey and Elliott were pleased with their morning's work and called the office in Belfast to let them know about the breakthrough. The team they left behind was not sitting back waiting for results from the boss; they, too, had made a crucial breakthrough that very day by finding two former residents who wanted to exorcise the ghosts of Kincora and were prepared to play an active part in the process. They might have been pleased to learn that because of their actions, that very night, 3 March 1980, was the last on which young men had to sleep inside Kincora. When Caskey and Elliott arrived back at Belfast International Airport Assistant Chief Constable Bill Meharg requested an urgent briefing with Caskey. The conversation did not last long. At its conclusion Meharg instructed Caskey immediately to get in touch with Dr Maurice Hayes, the Permanent Secretary at the Department of Health and Social Services.

Dr Hayes received the RUC officers at his Downpatrick home. He describes the circumstances of the urgent request from Caskey in his book *Minority Verdict: The Experiences of a Catholic Civil Servant* (The Blackstaff Press 1995)

> I was at a wake in Ardglass on a Friday evening when I got a call from Detective Caskey. He said he was at the airport and wished to see me immediately. He came to my home in Downpatrick and told me the result of his enquiries. He had just returned from interviewing a former Kincora boy who was now a male prostitute in London, and the youth had given him enough information to justify the laying of charges against the three top people in Kincora. He told me that I could not use the information directly since he had not yet reported to his super-

iors. The story he told was a chilling one in all its stark detail. It confirmed all our worst fears and the worst of the rumours that directly involved the home.

The next day, 4 March 1980, the three staff members concerned, Joseph Mains, Raymond Semple and William McGrath, were suspended from duty and Kincora was closed. The residents were immediately transferred to other accommodation.

As far as George Caskey was concerned, the gloves were off. He instructed his team of detectives to intensify the collection of statements and evidence against the Kincora staff. As soon as the staff members were suspended, a team of forensic scientists travelled to 236 Upper Newtownards Road to begin the process of gathering vital corroborating evidence which would later be used to secure convictions. Police investigators had great admiration for the team of scientific experts under the leadership of Richard Adams, for it took months of detailed searching and examination to persuade the old house to give up all its secrets.

In their first three days, however, Adams and his team had provided corroborating evidence which clearly indicated that boys in Kincora had taken part in homosexual relationships with McGrath and Mains. Because of legislation in Northern Ireland at the time which outlawed homosexuality, it was clear that some of the residents and former residents at Kincora had themselves broken the law. At this point Caskey took an important step to make possible the cooperation of boys who had lived in the hostel. He approached the then Director of Public Prosecutions, Sir Barry Shaw, who agreed that all those who made statements which by their nature implicated them in breaches of the law would be granted immunity from prosecution. They were thus free to make statements to police. Many of those interviewed admitted to being homosexual but, like Hugh Quinn, a large proportion told detectives their experiences in Kincora had led them into this type of lifestyle. The gathering of evidence in the form of statements from residents and former residents continued with some urgency and the attendant publicity about the hostel brought forward more and more individuals who saw that their complaints would finally be taken seriously. The result of all this activity was that by the end of March the investigators were ready to confront the three suspended staff members in RUC interview rooms.

In a coordinated operation, uniformed police officers gathered for a short briefing from plain-clothes investigators early on the morning of 1 April. Caskey and his team identified the three suspects they wanted to arrest that morning and gave details of the three addresses in different parts of the city to be visited at precisely the same time – 0800. Joe Mains, Raymond Semple and William McGrath were taken for questioning to the divisional police headquarters in the Kincora area, Mountpottinger RUC station. As one police source told me: 'We soon became aware of McGrath's political connections when we raided his home just down from the hostel on the Upper Newtownards Road and removed a number of political documents, some associated with Tara.'

For the next forty-eight hours the three men were

grilled about the allegations made against them. From the outset Mains and Semple admitted their offences but McGrath denied everything in spite of the overwhelming evidence confronting him. Even in the face of a mountain of damning evidence, McGrath was able to tell police the name of the organisation responsible for the false allegations against him. The interviewing officers were fascinated by the evidence of political intrigue evidenced by McGrath's counter-allegations. As the police were to discover, he had received the protection of the British secret service because for a number of years they put the integrity of the state above the abuse of boys in public care at Kincora.

14
STONEWALLING

Up to this point, William McGrath had successfully partitioned his life into separate compartments: the family man known to his wife and children was a different person to the McGrath of the Orange Lodge or the McGrath known to the terrified residents of Kincora, or to those who witnessed his politics of having a machine gun in one hand and a bible in the other, or indeed to those men with whom he had sexual relations. His arrest threw up the possibility that his whole duplicitous existence would be exposed to the gaze of all his family, friends and acquaintances. In custody, McGrath fiercely resisted police interrogation.

Number 188 Upper Newtownards Road is a tall brick building in the middle of a long row of terraced houses, only a few minutes walk away from Kincora at Number 236. Detective Sergeant Berkeley Elliott with Detective Sergeant Norman McLaughlin knocked on the front door of Number 188 that morning of 1 April 1980. The two detectives explained the nature of their early morning call and then searched McGrath's home, removing documents and pamphlets from a bedroom which McGrath told them he used as an office. Then they escorted him to Mountpottinger RUC station, where they arrived at 0850. The prisoner was taken to interview room Number 38 where he remained in the presence of one of the officers until interviewing got under way at 0940, after McGrath was cautioned. He made no reply. The detectives eased

McGrath into conversation by getting him to describe his work regime at Kincora. He explained that on four days of the week he worked from 0645 to 1200 or 1300 and on three days a night shift, from 1900 to midnight.

When the serious questioning began, McGrath quickly seized on what he described as the 'political' campaign against him.

> Police: Allegations have been made against you in the past?
> McGrath: The first time was ten years ago after I took over in Kincora. An anonymous letter or telephone call was made to Strandtown police who informed my headquarters – they got in touch with us. We had a conference with a Miss Wilson and Mr Mains.
> Police: What was the allegation?
> McGrath: That I was engaged in homosexual activity.
> Police: Were you?
> McGrath: It was a political attack.
> Police: Did you know by whom?
> McGrath: Yes, I thought the UVF.
> Police: Who?
> McGrath: I do not know.
> Police: Why?
> McGrath: I am in Tara and we are against all lawlessness around and we exposed ourselves to these people in the UVF.

(It was Garland who made the anonymous call that McGrath acknowledged, although he declined to explain in detail to the interviewing officers the true nature of the call.)

When McGrath mentioned the UVF to the interviewing officers he declined to inform them of the concerted campaign being run against him by that body in their monthly magazine *Combat*. McGrath was inviting such activity by his prolific letter-writing, which by the mid-1970s was accusing the UVF of being a communist organisation. In the September 1974 issue of *Combat*, for example, the UVF brigade staff went to the trouble of publishing a front-page rebuttal of allegations made in an anonymous letter to the *Belfast News Letter*. The UVF said the person responsible had himself been the victim of brainwashing by the degenerate hate-mongers of the UUUC and Tara Brigade. A few months later, in November 1974, the UVF brigade staff again returned to the subject of anti-UVF propaganda:

> Brigade pointed out that the vast majority of the anti-UVF propaganda was emanating from the DUP and Tara Brigade ... Brigade pointed out that the anti-UVF propaganda stems back to 1971, when hundreds of volunteers deserted Tara to join the UVF ... Regardless of whether we had a political wing or not, the black propagandists would still be operating against us.

When Caskey came into the room, he quickly turned the questioning around to the specific allegations made by Sammy, reading to McGrath Sammy's statement describing how McGrath threatened him with violence before raping him in the bathroom on the first landing.

> Caskey: What have you to say about that?
> McGrath: Unbelievable.
> Caskey: Do you think that these were proper things to do to a boy?
> McGrath; Very wrong to do.
> Caskey: How can you explain why a number of boys who never met each other should make similar allegations against you?
> McGrath: I do not know. It is a hazard of my job.
> Caskey: How do you explain these boys making similar allegations?
> McGrath: I cannot.
> Caskey: Several different police officers have interviewed these boys and have got the same picture of you interfering with them?
> McGrath: I cannot explain that.
> Caskey: Do you want all these boys to have to come into court and explain what you did to them?
> McGrath: There will be other stories come out in court.
> Caskey: What do you mean?
> McGrath: There will have to be a rebuttal to these allegations.
> Caskey: What do you mean?
> McGrath: We will have to deny them.
> Caskey: Can you provide us with details?
> McGrath: No I will not do that now.

In the early stages the police seemed to use a scatter-gun technique, switching the questioning from one set of allegations to another without warning, hoping to draw McGrath into acknowledgement or admission. He resisted with great skill, so much so that some of the officers who encountered him in the interrogation rooms were of the opinion that he had rehearsed this situation. Having led his personal and political life in so many sealed compartments clearly made it easier for him to maintain his position of indignant innocence.

When faced with allegations from a boy who accused McGrath of an act of sodomy and whose medical examination revealed that he had been engaged in anal intercourse, McGrath responded: 'That is understandable.'

>Police: Why?
>McGrath: Because he openly talked about his activities around the City Hall ... around the toilets.

The interrogation intensified, with McGrath using words like horrific to describe allegations made against him. Frequently, he would introduce a hint of political intrigue. For example, when asked to comment on a suggestion from some former residents that McGrath frightened boys into accepting his sexual advances, he replied: 'Why were they frightened of me? What threat had I over them? I have heard of a campaign about other organisations by certain people.' Asked what he meant, McGrath said: 'I will not say.' He was a little more forthcoming when the questioning turned to the subject of his abilities to provide a body massage, which many of the residents had referred to.

When shown a hand-written statement by Joe Mains which gave details of allegations by residents at the hostel, McGrath replied:

> McGrath: The part about the masseur business is correct. I did say that to him because it was part of my job as a hairdresser. I took a course in massage at Smae Institution, Leatherhead, Surrey before the war. I used to in my business as a hairdresser massage people's faces, necks and shoulders.
> Police: Is that correct?
> McGrath: Quite correct.
> Police: I never had a hairdresser massage me.
> McGrath: Well I have done it.
> Police: Did you massage [name of young man]'s shoulders?
> McGrath: It may have happened.

In another exchange McGrath tells his interrogators that he knew the source of earlier allegations and that 'they were out to destroy me'.

> Police: Are you prepared to name these people?
> McGrath: Not at the moment.
> Police: At what stage will you tell the police?
> McGrath: I will have to talk it over with my legal advisers. It is a new situation for me – I just do not know.
> Police: Bearing the seriousness of the allegations [in mind], don't you think it would be to your advantage if the police conducted investigations on

your behalf?

McGrath: If I was not convinced that you are satisfied that these allegations against me are true then I would consider that course of action.

Police: It is a serious matter if people conspire together to fabricate allegations of this nature. Don't you think such a serious matter should be investigated by the police?

McGrath: I think I know the original source of the allegations made ten years ago.

Police: What were these allegations?

McGrath: Simply that I was a homosexual.

Police: Were you a homosexual at that time?

McGrath: No.

Police: What form did the allegations take?

McGrath: A whispering campaign.

Police: You know the source of these allegations.

McGrath: Yes we do.

Police: Who's we?

McGrath: Those who know.

Police: Are you prepared to give the names of these other people against whom allegations have been made other than yourself?

McGrath: No.

Police: At what stage are you prepared to give these names?

McGrath: Later on, this will have to be discussed, you boys will have had your share.

Police: Are these people in high places?

McGrath: No higher than myself.

Police: Are they connected with Tara?

McGrath: Some of them.

Police: What reason is there for spreading such allegations?

McGrath: I think that will be brought out in the court.

Police: What is the reason for the allegations – political, religious or other?

McGrath: I should think it is political.

(McGrath explained that this attempt at character assassination would be earnestly challenged in the court, thereby exposing the fact that the 'Kincora boys' were jumping on the bandwagon.)

Police: As you say you know the source of ten years ago, did you ever consider legal action against the source?

McGrath: You can only take legal action against an individual and they wanted us to take action years ago.

Police: Who are they?

McGrath: That will not be told now because they would have got into the witness box and swore as much lies as these boys are telling now.

Police: Do I take that to mean that the allegations made ten years ago emanated from people who had been associating with you?

McGrath: Definitely not.

Police: Then why put them in the same class as the boys from Kincora?

McGrath: They were not boys, but we know that they

were prepared to swear our lives away as people and what we stood for.

Police: Surely it would be in your interest to tell the police their names and to have the matter investigated?

McGrath: No that needs to be reserved for the moment.

Police: Are you frightened?

McGrath: No, we will simply have a defence to prepare.

Police: To tell me now might prevent very serious charges being preferred against you at this stage.

McGrath: In the light of all you have said I can't believe that there is anything I could do to prevent this going to court.

Police: On the face of the evidence and the statements made by the boys from Kincora, the fact that you are not prepared to reveal what you consider vital information for your own defence would leave the police with little choice.

McGrath: What choice have I?

Over and over again, McGrath promised the interviewers that he would have his day in court when 'we' would have 'our defence' prepared. With the interviewers failing to breach his defences over many hours of questioning, McGrath must have felt himself grow stronger, so much so that before the day was over he made a remarkable arrangement. He agreed to a medical examination by the police doctor. He was taken to see Dr Robert Irwin at lunchtime on 2 April. By 2.55 pm he was facing the two sergeants in interview room Number 36. They had briefly chatted to Dr Irwin about the examination. The examination was to be a devastating blow for McGrath.

> Police: Dr Irwin is of the opinion that you have been a homosexual for some time and have had sex on many occasions and that you are a classic example of what he would expect to find, and his conclusion is quite clear.
> McGrath: Never, whatever the reason is for my physical condition, it is not that.
> Police: The doctor will say that the irritation close to your back passage is aggravated by homosexual intercourse.
> McGrath: Never. Never. I know it is ridiculous to fly in the face of medical evidence, there is no way whatever I have had sexual intercourse in my life. He is the expert, we have got to accept his conclusion.

(In his report Dr Irwin noted that McGrath seemed to be sexually stimulated during the examination of his penis. It increased in size and his right leg began to twitch uncontrollably. There was no escape from the doctor's conclusion which stated: 'I formed the opinion that this man had engaged in homosexual activity probably for some considerable time and that the findings and changes in his rectal area could not be put down to age, or to the fact that he had a pilonidul sinus operation; the salient points being the presence of the triangular scar at six o'clock and the radiating stria which folded in on themselves on rectal examination and the tendency of the rectum to gape on lateral pressure on the buttocks. The peculiar tremor observed in the right leg and the apparent sexual stimulation when handling his penis would indicate a high degree of homosexual activity, probably more in the active than the passive field.')

Attempting to appeal to McGrath's better nature, the police suggested that he should think of the poor children against whom he had offended and what he had done to them.

> McGrath: I don't worry because I have never done anything.
> Police: I don't know why you can't tell the truth.
> McGrath: I know my position.
> Police: What is your position?
> McGrath: I know that I never had sex with any person in my life, either giving or taking.
> Police: Do you accept Dr Irwin's evidence? He will say that he has examined up to twenty others in this case and you are the best example of a homosexual so far?
> McGrath: It is a mystery.

Even when confronted with the forensic evidence which showed that seminal stains were found at places inside Kincora where boys said McGrath had committed offences against them, he persisted in claiming innocence. Then there were the statements of admission of Mains and Semple. McGrath did not miss the point.

McGrath: There would appear to be corroboration. I appreciate everything you say but I know that I have never done the things of which I am accused.

As pressure mounted, McGrath accepted that things looked bad for him and told the police he would have to find some medical explanation for the doctor's conclusion. He concluded the interview by declaring: 'My final answer is a denial of all the allegations.' At 5.30 pm on 2 April, McGrath was taken to Townhall Street RUC station, where he was formally charged by Detective Inspector Caskey. These were little more than a specimen charges which would give the police more time to conduct the rigorous investigation promised by Caskey. Mains and Semple were held on similar charges at this time. It was to be twenty months until the court case. By this time the police had many more charges to put to McGrath and had widened the investigation to produce charges against three others involved in sexual abuse of young boys in other state-run residential homes. While the police continued their investigation, McGrath remained suspended from his duties at Kincora – on full pay – and therefore had more time to devote to his political cause. He was, after all, secretary of 'Ireland's Heritage' lodge that year.

On Friday 27 June McGrath read out to those present at the lodge meeting a letter from Charles Simpson seeking readmission to the lodge now that he had returned from Rhodesia. He was voted back into membership of a lodge which was obviously reeling from the effects of the charges facing McGrath. By September, when members were due to hold the annual election of office-bearers for

1981, William McGrath was moved to report that in spite of the low turnout for lodge meetings the members should still choose their leaders for the following year. Once the Worshipful Master and his Deputy had been elected, it was decided that all other officers be deemed re-elected. In the following month, at the meeting held on Friday 31 October, McGrath was back on familiar territory, urging the brethren 'to be much in prayer on behalf of the nation as there was some talk in high places of a change in the name of the RUC and of Éire returning to the Commonwealth as part of the price for a change in the Act of Settlement.' The 'doomsday' mentality clearly still prevailed as 1980 drew to a close and Northern Ireland prepared for one of the most troubled years in the continuing conflict.

1981 was the year Ray Smallwoods of the UDA led an armed gang in an unsuccessful attempt to murder Bernadette McAliskey and Paisley set out on a series of demonstrations as part of his Carson Trail campaign which included a walk up a County Antrim hillside with five hundred men waving firearms certificates. Most important of all, it was the year of the hunger strikes by Republican prisoners at the Maze, which resulted in ten men starving themselves to death in order to pressurise the British into reinstating political status in Northern Ireland jails. The election of hunger striker Bobby Sands as the Westminster MP for Fermanagh-South Tyrone gave rise to renewed political ambition on the part of Sinn Féin. At the party's Ard Fheis on 31 October Danny Morrison confirmed its intention of contesting all future elections: 'Who here really believes we can win the war through the ballot box?

But will anyone here object if, with a ballot paper in one hand and the Armalite in the other, we take power in Ireland?' (Reported in *An Phoblacht/Republican News*, 5 November 1981)

The day before Morrison's address in Dublin, the monthly meeting of Ireland's Heritage Lodge took place in Belfast. So poor was the attendance that the existing office bearers were simply re-elected, McGrath maintaining his position as secretary. As the Worshipful District Master, Brother Jack Galbraith, joined the meeting to conduct the election of officers, he urged the lodge to maintain its witness despite all the difficulties it had to face. From his new home at Ballyhalbert, a small village on the County Down coast, McGrath carried on with his duties to the lodge as if nothing had happened and took the time to send a letter out to every member of the lodge appealing for a good turnout at the October meeting. This is what he had to say to his fellow Orangemen:

> Dear Sir & Brother
>
> It is with a heavy heart that I write these lines to each member of our Lodge. The last meeting we had was in the month of June. No meeting was arranged for July. In August only three members turned up so no meeting could be held. In September the same three Brethren attended despite the fact that all the members were circulated calling them to an Election of Officers! Again no meeting and not a single apology received. Really, it is not good enough.
>
> What has happened to us that such a state of affairs can exist among us? There is no doubt but

that such apathy will bring spiritual and political death to all we hold dear in our beloved land. The most precious thing we possess is our spiritual and political freedom, but a price has to be paid for that freedom! Attendance at our Lodge and the constant performance of the vows we have made as Orangemen is a vital part of that price. Without these things we do not deserve to survive as a people.

Again I say, what has happened to us? Have we forgotten the glory that filled our souls as we unfurled our new Banner so many years ago, a banner that was to become the most publicised banner of all time? Have we forgotten the deep emotion that welled up within us as we paraded the Flags of the four Provinces of Ireland down the aisle of St Mary's Church for dedication, and in doing so laid claim to all the territory the enemy had taken from us in the past? Has something died within us that these things mean so little now?

Our next meeting will be held (D.V.) on Friday, 30 October at 7.30 pm. in Clifton Street Orange Hall. Please note the time and plan to attend.

The monthly November meeting of the lodge took place on Friday 27 November, by which time the IRA had murdered South Belfast MP, Reverend Robert Bradford, who had attended meetings in McGrath's house years before. The meeting condemned his murder and offered prayers to his family. McGrath might not have realised it at the time but this was to be his last appearance at a lodge meeting. For as Ireland's Heritage Lodge struggled to survive the scandal of William McGrath, the RUC were travelling the world in pursuit of evidence with which to convict him. Caskey's detectives were busy tracing former residents of Kincora in the United States, Australia and various parts of Europe. As Christmas 1981 approached, the day of reckoning for the six defendants was approaching. McGrath maintained his innocence, seemingly determined to have his day in court. His opportunity came on Thursday, 10 December 1981, the day before his sixty-fifth birthday, when, along with the five other defendants he stood before the Lord Chief Justice Lord Lowry in Courtroom Number 1 at Belfast Crown Court.

The involvement in a sex scandal of McGrath, a prominent Orangeman and leader of the strange paramilitary group Tara, had whetted the public's appetite, and even before the case opened on 10 December reporters were busy gathering information about McGrath. I sat in the packed press gallery as the six defendants stood in the dock listening to the catalogue of accusations against them. Each in turn admitted his guilt, except of course McGrath, who denied all the charges put to him. There were four of buggery, six of gross indecency, seven of indecent assault and one of attempted buggery. A few people in the public gallery watched as the five others were removed from the dock for sentencing later and the court prepared to hear the evidence against McGrath. Among them were one or two of those he had abused, including Sammy, who were permitted to leave the small room where police were keeping the vast majority of witnesses in the case. Pencils were sharpened in anticipation of a fascinating case, and once the court had been cleared of the other defendants those present hung on every word that came from the lips of John Creaney QC as he gave his opening address.

I delivered the following account of the day's proceedings on the evening news programme on BBC:

> In opening the case against McGrath Mr John Creaney QC said the Kincora home was a hostel for the accommodation of boys aged between fifteen and eighteen who were in need of care and protection. They were sent there either by the juvenile courts or because they were not receiving proper care or attention at home – or if they were exposed to moral danger. McGrath started working at the hostel in June 1971 and his duties were supervisory and to some extent administrative. Mr Creaney said that eleven persons had made allegations of sexual misconduct against them by McGrath. The misconduct against the boys began shortly after he started working at the hostel and Mr Creaney said it had continued right up to the time of his suspension in January [it was actually March] last year. The court was told that McGrath had engaged in mild and gross acts of indecency and Mr Creaney said that in some instances the evidence will be that he compelled or threatened the youths. Evidence would show that there had been a systematic corruption of boys who are now grown men and who were under the care and control of McGrath. Mr Creaney said the indecent activity took place in the boys' bedrooms in the mornings before they got

up, while they were watching television, in the toilets and on the landing of the first floor at the hostel. Mr Creaney appealed to the jury that although they would be dealing with issues and evidence which would be abhorrent and distasteful to them, not to allow this to affect their judgement in any way. Earlier former warden Joseph Mains and his deputy Raymond Semple admitted ten charges between them, involving sexual offences, and they have now been put back for sentencing. The case continues tomorrow.

Any hopes harboured by members of LOL 1303 that their leader would produce a defence to clear his name and that of the lodge were dealt a fatal blow next morning in Court Number 1. For instead of presenting a stout defence revealing a conspiracy against him by politically motivated opponents, McGrath's barrister Desmond Boal stunned everyone present by announcing that his client wished to be rearraigned. McGrath stood as once again the charges were put to him, although it was soon clear that some of those put to him the previous day had been removed. He replied 'guilty' to two charges of buggery, five of gross indecency and eight of indecent assault. Overnight it seemed, something, or someone, had influenced McGrath to change his pleas to guilty. The Lord Chief Justice adjourned the court so he could prepare his judgement. Five days later, on Wednesday, 16 December, he sentenced the six men before the court, dealing first with the three from Kincora. He described their activities as 'loathsome and perverted behaviour between young men and boys.

The Kincora three had admitted a total of twenty-five sexual offences against eleven boys at the home between 1960 and 1980. Mains was jailed for six years on two charges of buggery, three of gross indecency and one of indecent assault. Semple received five years on four charges of buggery and gross indecency. McGrath was jailed for four years.

There were sighs of disappointment over his sentence in another part of Crumlin Road Courthouse that day, in the room where more than thirty witnesses awaited the outcome of the trial which they had made possible because of their courage in making statements to the police. One of the most disappointed was Sammy, who had kept one matter secret from the investigating officers. A few days before the case began he had been walking to the home of his foster parents in Newtownards. A large car drew up alongside him as he reached the front door. Two large men in black leather jackets were sitting in the back seat. One of them said: 'There's someone who wants to talk to you! Do you think you have a nice face?' Sammy told them he had nothing to say to them. The passenger's window was wound down. The street lighting revealed inside the familiar face of William McGrath. He leaned forward and spoke to the startled youth on the pavement: 'If you know what is for your own good, shut your mouth!' Sammy bravely stood his ground, shouting back that he had said all he had to say to the police and that he had given them statements. He found it difficult to make out what McGrath mumbled under his breath before the car sped off. For Sammy, the most sinister aspect of this frightening episode was the fact that the car was in his street at all. He lived in a part of town which was located behind the security barriers which were locked each night by the security forces as a means of keeping car bombs out of the town centre. Sammy said there was normally a policeman nearby. He ran after the car but by the time he reached the top of his street and turned the corner the car had disappeared from view, no doubt making its way back to Belfast. And the security gate was closed and locked.

Behind bars at Belfast's Crumlin Road Prison, McGrath had time to reflect on his life. The news bulletins in the first few weeks of 1982 were preoccupied with the demise of the John De Lorean factory at Dunmurry and details of a committee of enquiry into the Kincora scandal announced by Secretary of State James Prior. McGrath was busy tidying up some paperwork of his own. On 19 January, prisoner 3422 composed a letter which must have caused him great pain. It was addressed to the Secretary of Ireland's Heritage Lodge, LOL 1303:

> Dear Sir and Brother
> Owing to my present circumstances I wish to tender my resignation from LOL 1303 and from the Orange Institution. It is with a heavy heart that I take this step for the high ideals behind the formation of our Lodge are more precious to me now than ever before. I charge you therefore, one and all, before God that you not only maintain 1303 as an effective part of our great Institution but that you exert every possible effort to build up its numbers so that it will increasingly become a power for good in the

Institution and outside.

May I take this opportunity to say that never at any time or in any way have I committed an act 'unbecoming an Orangeman'. You can be assured of that. In this whole business I have a conscience void of offence towards God and towards man, a heart at peace with itself and best of all the Lord is with me. Greetings in Chirst to all the Brethren and may the Lord be with you all. I would value your prayers.
Yours faithfully
William McGrath

If McGrath nurtured any hope that the Lodge might rally behind him and beg him not to resign, he was to be sadly disappointed. Ten days after McGrath wrote his letter, the Lodge met at Clifton Street Orange Hall. As they gathered to consider the resignation of their founding member, a few miles away on the other side of the city gunmen from the INLA shot dead John McKeague in his shop on the Beersbridge Road, the shop where he used to accept plain brown envelopes containing cash from his Army Intelligence handlers. The Worshipful Master of Ireland's Heritage Lodge informed those present that McGrath had offered his resignation. Unfortunately, he told them, in the present sad circumstances and because of previous events it was not possible to accept the resignation. There was, he explained, no alternative but to pass a motion of expulsion. Such a motion was proposed by David Hanna and seconded by R. Stewart. It was passed unanimously, according to the records. Two District Officers (Number 3 District) were then permitted to join the meeting to preside over the installation of officers. One of them, Brother J. Galbraith, spoke of his sorrow over recent events and concluded by expressing his 'complete confidence' in McGrath's son Worthington, who it appears was present at the meeting which recorded the unanimous vote to expel McGrath. The meeting could not now continue without taking time for a brief discussion about the future of the Lodge. Chaplain David Kerr referred to the stigma now associated with the name and number of the Lodge. He offered three options for consideration:

1 To continue as at present, which he personally believed was not possible
2 To reform with a new name and number, which he thought was impracticable
3 To disband

Members of the lodge voted unanimously to disband by handing in the warrant of the lodge to the District. The next meeting of LOL 1303 was fixed for 26 February and this – as things turned out – was the last meeting of Ireland's Heritage Lodge. The decision to disband was confirmed by all present at this meeting and it was decided that the union flag, pole and strap, as well as the spare pole be given to St Mary's 72nd Boys' Brigade Company, after advice had been sought of the District Officers. The District Master Dawson Bailie and his deputy Richard Crothers were admitted to the meeting to be formally told of the disbandment of the lodge. The District Officers urged the lodge members to consider reforming under a new name and number but as McGrath's son

Worthington told them, they would still be open to attack from 'malicious elements'. It was made clear that it was not just the bad publicity which was forcing the lodge to disband, but also the falling attendances. Of fifteen members currently on the books, only seven were considered to be active. By six votes to one [R. Stewart voted against], this small band of Orangemen removed Ireland's Heritage Lodge from the register at the House of Orange in Belfast. The lodge had £120 in the bank and it was decided to meet for a farewell dinner at La Mon House Hotel on Friday, March 12. 'Doomsday' for Ireland's Heritage Lodge had arrived in a most unexpected manner.

Part VI
Establishing the Truth
1982-95

15
Intimate Ties

William McGrath maintained almost total public silence over the Kincora affair until his death in 1991. He did issue a statement from his prison cell a few months after he had been convicted:

> With reference to Dr Paisley's statement at a press conference concerning the Kincora affair, it is of such a nature that it demands an answer. The following are the facts. Never have I been asked to speak in a Free Presbyterian Church, nor has it been suggested that I should do so. The question of being banned does not therefore arise.
>
> For a number of years the Orange lodge to which I belong was kindly granted the use of John Knox Memorial Free Presbyterian Church for a parade and service each November. I was responsible for organising all these services. On one such occasion I had

the honour of acting as chairman at the service. All this was with the full knowledge and approval of Dr Paisley, Mr James Heyburn, his secretary and the church committee.

Some five years ago this parade and service were cancelled for no reason other than the Free Presbyterian Church decided that only Free Presbyterian ministers would be allowed into their pulpit and refused us the right to invite clergy of other denominations to address us. We felt as a lodge that this was a surrender of spiritual liberty that we were not prepared to make and so plans for all future services were cancelled by the lodge.

Dr Paisley and the Reverend Martin Smyth share in a common condemnation. They both claim that they knew I was a homosexual. If these two gentlemen had been true to their high and holy calling as pastors of God's flock, they would have sought to restore me in the spirit of meekness.

They had ample opportunity of doing so over many years, bound to me as they were, the one by the most sacred of Orange oaths, the other by intimate family ties in the Free Presbyterian Church and in the DUP. Instead by their public pronouncements they aid and abet those who would silence the Gospel that I have tried to make over a lifetime, and they gave succour and support to those who would destroy the fight for faith and freedom to which I have made some little contribution.

Further, five of us were convicted for alleged similar offences, yet I am the only one that has been singled out and attacked. Every intelligent person will ask himself, 'Why this vendetta? Why this persecution of one individual? Finally I challenge anyone to prove:

1 That I was involved in a vice ring at Kincora or elsewhere.
2 That I recruited young people for prostitution.
3 That I was in contact with politicians, businessmen or others for this purpose.
4 That I received payment or reward for such services.

The statement was issued through McGrath's solicitor on 2 March 1982 – just two days before Mr Smyth won the Westminster by-election for South Belfast. It was released to the media three months after McGrath had been jailed and less than two months after a news conference called by Paisley on 26 January. The Free Presbyterian Church leader was attempting to use this news conference to steal the thunder of two *Irish Times* reporters, Ed Moloney and Andy Pollak, who had prepared a story which would raise questions about Mr Paisley's links with the convicted sex offender. It was a tactic he had used successfully in the past: identify an issue with potential for causing embarrassment and stage a loud media event with theatrical bluster in order to intimidate the press. However, while Paisley might have found the link with McGrath embarrassing, there is no evidence or suggestion that he was aware that McGrath or other staff members were abusing boys at Kincora.

This particular piece of Paisley theatre was staged

because Moloney and Pollak had been talking to Valerie Shaw, once a missionary in Paisley's church, and had learned of her attempts prior to 1980 to alert the DUP leader to McGrath's corrupting sexual influence. Seasoned political commentators later agreed it was not one of Paisley's finest hours as he fumbled through the barrage of questions from assembled media people. Naturally he disputed Miss Shaw's version of events and I watched him turn under pressure to his general secretary James Heyburn to seek assistance with certain answers. This news conference is worthy of close scrutiny as it proved to be a springboard for months of investigation by reporters keen to cross-check the points made by the DUP leader. This is the text of Paisley's statement:

> Yesterday afternoon Ed Moloney and someone else from *The Irish Times* called at my home. I was actually resting for I had been to Canada and I was suffering from jet lag and I had had a heavy day on the Sunday. So I was actually in bed all day yesterday resting. But evidently these two gentlemen were very keen to see me and we talked, as I am sure Ed will confirm, by intercom. They asked me the following questions: Number one, did I know anything about Kincora? And I said I knew nothing about Kincora. They said, did I know a homosexual called Mr McGrath and I said I had no comment to make on that. They then said that Miss Shaw, who had left the employment of this Church partly in protest, had informed me about happenings in Kincora. You will confirm that Ed? [Answer: 'No I

asked you whether Miss Shaw had told you about McGrath being a homosexual which is entirely different from knowing about the events at Kincora.'] I am not going to enter into a discussion about your questions. That was my understanding of it and Sergeant Taylor was present.

I asked these men would they not come back today and they said No. They wanted to see me later on that afternoon and I told them I was resting up and was not seeing anybody. Now let me fill you in on the background: Some years ago the Free Presbyterian Church of Ulster purchased Cliftonville Irish Presbyterian Church and it is now the John Knox Free Presbyterian Church. After it had been purchased I was approached by the Orange Lodge known as Ireland's Heritage Lodge and they asked me could they run an Orange service in the church. I consented and gave them permission to have this service and I consulted my officers here as at that time John Knox Memorial Free Presbyterian Church was under the jurisdiction of this church (Martyrs Memorial) and I was in charge of the church at this time. Mr McGrath who has since been imprisoned for actions in Kincora was very active in this lodge and took a leading part in the organisation of this service.

Some time after the first service occurred at the church Miss Shaw, who was a missionary to the Jews and an employee of this church approached me. She said that she had evidence that McGrath was a homosexual and she produced a letter written to what I will call a Mr 'X' and the reason why I am not naming this person is because this man is now a happily married man and a family man. But Miss Shaw, who lives in Voltaire Gardens and is the woman who put out the statement originally – no doubt she will be prepared to give you more information because she is the person who brought about this press conference – she produced this letter to Mr 'X' from Mr McGrath and this letter had some undertones of homosexuality about it. I said I would like to meet Mr 'X' and Mr 'X' came to the church here and I met him. He said he had been corrupted by Mr McGrath. I asked would he face McGrath and he said certainly not. I then said to him, 'You put me in a great difficulty because you have made a very serious accusation, the person you accuse is going to preside at an Orange service at one of my churches and I am not in a position to bring you face to face.' He said on no account would he be prepared to face Mr McGrath. So I then was in a great difficulty. My difficulty was that I had heard a serious accusation about a person who was not a member of my Church but who was going to preside at an Orange service at one of my churches and I was not in a position to face him with the evidence.

I consulted with my office bearers and we decided that I should meet Mr McGrath and I met him in this room accompanied by my general secretary Mr James Heyburn. I put to him the accusations which had been made. I, of course, named the person that had made the accusation, named the letter he had written, a letter by the way which I have not in my possession for Miss Shaw asked me to give it back to her – and I faced him. And he said to me what I thought he would say, 'Where is the man who made the accusation? Why will he not come and make the accusation face to face?' I said to him: 'Mr McGrath, this accusation is of a very serious nature. I understand the feelings of the person who has made it and as far as I am concerned I have to to make a decision and my decision is that you will not be welcome in any pulpit in the Free Presbyterian Church and I am informing the lodge concerned that the service would go ahead under one condition. That you have no part or lot in that service.'

Certain friends of Mr McGrath in Ireland's Heritage Lodge were very angry. They suggested first of all that they would cancel the meeting. They even suggested they would picket the church. But I remained adamant and I said on no account would Mr McGrath be at any Free Presbyterian pulpit. The service went ahead and Mr McGrath took no part in the service. And there the matter rested as far as my Church and myself are concerned. At no time did Miss Shaw make any accusations to me about happenings at Kincora. If she had made such accusations I would have advised her to go to the police or I would have gone to the police myself. But Miss Shaw has visited quite a number of ministers of various denominations for when the police made investigations about the Kincora case after my

Parliamentary colleague, Mr Peter Robinson, raised it in the House of Commons with my support, the police called with these ministers as they also called upon me. And I made to them a similar statement as I have made to you today. Miss Shaw had a serious doctrinal disagreement with this church... and she resigned and her resignation was accepted. And that, gentlemen, is my statement.

By issuing this statement Ian Paisley hoped to end all speculation about the extent of his knowledge of William McGrath and Kincora. But the significance of the statement is not so much what it contains as what it omits. There is no mention of dates, and Miss Shaw and Garland were quick to allege it contained inaccuracies. Garland provided me with a detailed written statement for the purposes of this book, in order yet again to rebut Paisley's statement. He states that he made many attempts between 1971 and 1974 to inform Paisley of his concerns about McGrath. He maintains that he never claimed to anyone that he had been corrupted, for the simple reason that he had not. Garland continues: 'Ian's reference to my marriage was disingenuous as well as being irrelevant. I had been married almost thirteen years before he made the statement. Finally, with reference to Paisley's protestation that he never knew that McGrath worked in Kincora: 'Paisley lived only a few hundred yards from McGrath's home and from Kincora. It seemed inconceivable that he knew nothing about McGrath's employment there.'

It was clear from the question and answer session that followed the statement that the media were not convinced by Paisley's performance. Pressed by reporters, Paisley revealed that he knew McGrath when he ran Faith House at Finaghy (the late 1950s) and that McGrath had accompanied him and others on a delegation about security policy to Northern Ireland Prime Minister James Chichester-Clark in the 1960s [in fact 1969]. The main issues that arose from this news conference concerned the date at which Miss Shaw complained to Mr Paisley, his repeated assertions that he did not know where McGrath worked and his statement during questioning that the DUP leader had taken a decision that no member of Tara could be a member of his party.

Miss Shaw and Paisley do not dispute the fact that she told the DUP leader of her concerns about McGrath being homosexual but they are at odds over the details of the conversation and when it took place. Miss Shaw says it was on Monday 28 October 1973 that she first raised the matter with Paisley, following a chat the previous week with a lay preacher from south-east Belfast who expressed his concerns about McGrath working in Kincora at a time when his homosexuality was known to a number of people in the city. According to Miss Shaw, the next day [29 October] a member of the Free Presbyterian Church, who went on to become a minister in the church, showed her a handbill advertising a service of Ireland's Heritage Orange Lodge at a Free Presbyterian Church in North Belfast the following Sunday which would be 'assisted by Brother William McGrath'. I have a copy of that handbill which states that the service was to take place at 3 pm on that Sunday 4 November, the main speaker the Reverend G. H. Mason 'assisted by Brother William McGrath, LOL

1303.' Underneath this information is a classic piece of McGrathism: 'Romanism and Communism are on the march! Slowly but surely the once beautiful district of Duncairn and Cliftonville are [*sic*] becoming a slum. We urge you to stand your ground and frustrate the enemy's plans. Turn out in your thousands for this parade and help keep your district PROTESTANT! Parade will be headed by the Union Flag and the historic Flags of the Four Provinces of Ireland.

Paisley insisted that he saw Miss Shaw not in 1973 but about a year later, and he flatly rejected her claim that she mentioned Kincora. Neither did he mention that he had been told about McGrath even before Miss Shaw came to see him, by Dave in 1971. Paisley insisted that he did not know McGrath was employed in Kincora; he simply did not know where McGrath was employed:

> Question: When was all this?
> Paisley: 1955, sorry 1975.
> Question: Were you aware at the time that McGrath was working in Kincora?
> Paisley: No. I did not even know where he worked.

Later Paisley said he did not know 'anything about Kincora or McGrath until it broke'.

Seated just behind Paisley was his church secretary James Heyburn, someone who knew McGrath well enough to attend meetings in McGrath's home and to sign as guarantor for a loan to buy a printer for use by Tara. Heyburn was adamant that he did not know of McGrath's homosexuality. The aim of the press conference was to put as much distance as possible between Paisley and the convicted sex offender.

For weeks after the news conference I continued to dig around, becoming more and more fascinated by McGrath's political connections and the apparent interest of the British intelligence services. It was during this period that I made something of a breakthrough when I found out that two of McGrath's children had been married in the Free Presbyterian Martyrs Memorial Church on the Ravenhill Road in Belfast, the headquarters of Paisley's own church. The marriage certificates of both Worthington and Elizabeth McGrath revealed that the officiating clergyman was one Ian Paisley. These facts had not been volunteered by Paisley at his news conference, which was held in a room at the same church on the Ravenhill Road.

On 25 February 1982 I obtained copies of the marriage certificates from the official registration office in Belfast. The first wedding, that of McGrath's son William Worthington and Dora Dorothy Haire, took place on 15 June 1971. On the certificate McGrath's home address is given as 4 Greenwood Avenue, off the Upper Newtownards Road, and William McGrath's occupation is given as 'clerk.' McGrath's other son Harvey Andrew was a witness, along with Roberta Lunn. The second certificate is for the marriage of McGrath's daughter Elizabeth Jean Frances to Francis Millar on 22 January 1976. The McGraths' home address is given as 188 Upper Newtownards Road and William McGrath's stated occupation is given as 'welfare officer.'

I was immediately struck by the thought that any minister involved in marrying the children of a man who had been such an active friend in politics going back many years would surely know something about the man and his family, would surely have had some idea of what the man did for a living. After all McGrath had been a member of the Paisley-led delegation which went to see Prime Minister Chichester-Clark in 1969, had visited Paisley's home in the company of members of Tara such as Garland, in 1966 had gone to warn him that certain individuals were linking him with the UVF and had recruited men with him at the very church where the weddings had taken place. Yet at his news conference, Paisley chose not to reveal that he had married two of McGrath's children in his church – and one of the weddings had taken place after, on Paisley's own admission, Miss Shaw had told him about McGrath. As a result Paisley claimed that he had personally confronted McGrath (whom he was frequently heard to call 'Billy') about serious allegations concerning his sexuality and told McGrath he would not be permitted to take part in the Gunpowder Plot services in the Free Presbyterian John Knox Church.

When I returned to the office that day I showed the marriage certificates to my bosses and they agreed that this was significant, given what Paisley had said at his news conference and now knowing some of what he chose not to say. They instructed me to continue working over the weekend to build towards a special report on the teatime television news on the Monday evening, 1 March.

It turned out to be a very busy weekend. On Friday 26 February Garland got in touch with me and told me a London Sunday paper was planning to name him over the weekend. I had been in contact with Garland for many weeks but had agreed to conceal his name – you will have noted that Paisley referred to Garland as Mr 'X', and that is how he had been known in the media. But he said he wanted to feel in control of his own destiny and if he was going to be forced out into the open he would rather choose the time and place. We therefore agreed to do a television interview on camera next day, the Saturday, at the BBC offices. With Garland forced into going public there was one other element of the story which could now be told. Some time earlier Garland let me see a copy of the loan McGrath received for the printing machine, but because his name was prominent I could not use the document. Now this was going to be possible and it was going to reveal Paisley's secretary Heyburn as a guarantor. The BBC's head of News and Current Affairs at the time was an Englishman, Stephen Claypole, his deputy a local man, John Conway. All agreed on the Friday that I should work all weekend towards a lengthy report for the Monday programme, possibly a piece of ten minutes duration. In order to assist me they told me they would release another reporter – Peter Gould – to help on the Sunday.

Filming took place on the Saturday, when Roy Garland came to the BBC and before doing an interview read a prepared statement seated in front of a film camera. We then did an interview about his life and times in Tara and his association with McGrath. On the teatime television news that Saturday evening we ran the story about Mr 'X' going public on his allegations about William McGrath and Kincora. I believe it was the lead story although I cannot be absolutely certain.

There was much more to do that weekend. I visited Dave at his home, to firmly establish his views about

McGrath and the actions he claims he took. Peter Gould accompanied me on this visit and heard what Dave had to say. He also accompanied me on my second visit to James Heyburn's home although we did not go inside, and Peter waited at the gate of the house while I spoke to Heyburn at his front door. I had called to Heyburn earlier on and spent some time in his house discussing his knowledge of Tara and McGrath. On 24 February, Heyburn sent me a letter on Martyrs Memorial Church headed paper and on the Monday morning we had prepared it in the BBC to show on screen in the form of a caption:

> Further to your visit to my home last night I now wish to put on record my response. Dr Paisley and the Free Presbyterian Church campaigned from the very beginning for a Public Sworn Inquiry. This they have now achieved. They will defend themselves at the inquiry and give the lie to Miss Shaw's accusations.
>
> The Public Sworn Inquiry is a proper forum for a full investigation, not the bias [sic] programmes which the BBC has sponsored and for which you are partly responsible.

The letter claimed that the *Nationwide* broadcast had deliberately failed to refer to the reason for Miss Shaw's resignation because this would have made clear that her resignation was unconnected to the allegations about Kincora. It went on 'The *Nationwide* programme cut out entirely Dr Paisley's call for the Public Sworn Inquiry and also concealed the nature of Miss Shaw's resignation. I am prepared to let the matter rest and have no comment to make until then.'

The letter is signed J. A. B. Heyburn, General Secretary.

I spent time with a film editor choosing the clips of Garland's interview and statement for insertion in a report which I would link in the studio. The report was to be recorded on VT (video tape) for transmission on *Scene Around Six*. As I typed out my script in the reporters' room, the pages were taken immediately to Claypole's office where he and a BBC solicitor from London carefully read them. By late afternoon I had finished writing and a newsroom secretary had processed the script which she then ran off on a copier. Before the recording there was to be a viewing in the film editor's cutting room. There was considerable excitement in the newsroom about the story, which looked as though it might run for almost twelve minutes.

Film editor Ray Allen had spliced the selected clips on to one reel and we were ready for the screening in front of the BBC management. Present in the cutting room were Stephen Claypole, Head of News and Current Affairs; John Conway, his deputy; Cecil Taylor, Head of Programmes; Don Anderson, Head of Radio; the BBC's London solicitor and I. I read the script and on cue, Ray played in the clips of interview. At its conclusion there was a discussion about the appropriateness of running with the story. Initially I was alarmed at the tone of the conversation although I suspected we were simply playing devil's advocate, looking at what might happen in the worst case scenario. But the longer the discussion continued, the more alarmed I became. There were few people in the room speaking up in favour of showing the item at all, and, amazingly, the very people who had encouraged me to work all weekend on this 'special' report which we had flagged at the end of the Saturday news story, were now ambivalent, to say the least. Programme time loomed and if we were going to drop the story, the news producer had to be informed so that other material could replace it. In the end someone, I cannot remember who, suggested we take a show of hands. This was incredible to me. Even more unbelievable was the vote. Only two people in that room voted in favour of transmitting the report. The second person was Don Anderson.

I was amazed and utterly confused. In my opinion too much attention was paid to the London solicitor who because he had not been present for the story from the beginning viewed the material as dangerous, fearing it might be seen as a gratuitous attack on Paisley. Even though it was pointed out several times that Paisley had had an opportunity to reveal the details of the wedding at his news conference but had chosen not to, and even though it was pointed out that by holding the news conference Paisley had thrown his role in the whole affair into the public arena, the solicitor could not be moved. I left the cutting room in disgust.

Although I was desperately disappointed by the refusal of the BBC to run with the marriage certificates story, I continued working on Kincora. Some time after this I discovered *News Letter* advertisements for the annual Gunpowder Plot Service of Ireland's Heritage Lodge to take place at Paisley's church and I confronted the DUP leader with them one morning after a press conference at the

Park Avenue Hotel in East Belfast to mark the return of a unionist delegation from the United States. I have since uncovered a considerable amount of documentary evidence regarding these parades, such as the letter sent to the Lodge on 4 July 1973 informing them that the request for use of the church would be put before the 'session and committee' as soon as possible. The letter was signed by Heyburn, who wished Ireland's Heritage every success on the Twelfth. The notification of the 1974 service makes interesting reading: lodge secretary Worthington McGrath wrote: 'The Preacher on this occasion will be the Reverend Dr Ian R. K. Paisley, MP, assisted by Brother Frank Millar, LOL 1303.'

By 1978, Ireland's Heritage LOL 1303 was beginning to experience difficulties in gaining access to Paisley's John Knox Church for the annual November Gunpowder Plot service. On 25 October 1978, McGrath himself, as lodge secretary, was compelled to write to District Officers (Number 3 District) informing them of the cancellation of the service. He explained that on May 22 he had written to the Reverend David Creane, Minister of the John Knox Church, enclosing a cheque for the proposed use of the church on Sunday, 5 November. According to McGrath this letter was not even acknowledged so another letter was sent to Mr Creane in 'mid-September' seeking confirmation of the booking before the next lodge meeting on 29 September. Again, McGrath reported, there was no reply. He then wrote: 'On 27 September we phoned the Reverend David Creane who informed us the Church Committee would not meet till [sic] late the following week. Mr Creane promised to phone us as soon as the meeting was over.

To date no phone call or letter has been received. In view of these facts you will realise that we had no alternative but to cancel our Service.'

We have evidence here of the first difficulties faced by McGrath and his lodge over use of Paisley's Free Presbyterian Church. McGrath wrote: 'Our Parade was never a large Parade by any standard, but we believe it was an important Parade in that it kept open a district that is rapidly being over-run by the enemy. After five years of effort by our Lodge that advantage has now been lost, not through any fault of the Lodge or of the Orange Institution, but through the unbusinesslike methods, the could not care less attitude and the complete lack of co-operation on the part of the Free Presbyterian Church.' Clearly, McGrath did not associate this difficulty with the growing knowledge of his own homosexual demeanour which had, according to Paisley, been the subject of discussion with the leader of the Free Presbyterian Church a few years earlier.

While the Free Presbyterian Church did not feel free to explain why they did not want McGrath speaking from one of their pulpits at this point in 1978, things did begin to change the following year when during an exchange of correspondence with McGrath (still lodge secretary), the secretary of the John Knox Church, R. Wylie, informed McGrath that the service could go ahead on Sunday, 4 November only on condition there was a Free Presbyterian Minister, 'to protect our testimony'. In his letter of 30 June, Wylie reminded McGrath of the stand taken by the Free Presbyterian Church against apostasy and ecumenism. On 18 July, McGrath replied, seeking clarification and reminding Wylie that 'in the past we have had a preacher in your pulpit who was not a Free Presbyterian.' He sought a 'clear ruling' at an early date. It came a week later when Wylie informed McGrath that the church committee had decided that the 'only preacher acceptable on this occasion would be one from the Free Presbyterian Church.' Wylie added: 'We know that your lodge is made up of members of all the Protestant denominations. However, this is a Free Presbyterian Church and because of the stand our church takes against popery, apostasy and ecumenism we feel that is the religious climate that prevails in our country today, the only way to protect our testimony in these matters would be to have a Free Presbyterian Minister.' This did not go down well with the Ireland's Heritage Lodge.

On 22 September, McGrath responded to Wylie, notifying him of cancellation of the service due to the conditions on worship being imposed by the Free Presbyterian Church. As he put it in the letter: 'We have no objection whatever to sitting under the ministry of a Free Presbyterian Minister, but after prayerful consideration our lodge feels that we cannot accept this as an imposed condition of worship. Our lodge is convinced that the acceptance of such a condition would:

1 Be a denial of spiritual liberty.
2 Be an insult to the men of God in other denominations.
3 We believe the Doctrine of Separation is no longer a valid claim in the Free Presbyterian Church since its Moderator, Reverend Dr Ian. R. K. Paisley, sits in the Common Market which is the economic and political

arm of the same evil system of which the World Council of Churches is the spiritual arm.'

McGrath was clearly taking a swipe at his former friend and ally. It seems that McGrath's sexual orientation had finally broken up another friendship. At the lodge meeting on Friday 28 September, McGrath read this letter to those members present as the lodge's response to Wylie. It is recorded that the lodge 'should explore the possibility of another venue for the service in future years.' But there was no need, for by November 1980 McGrath was already suspended from his duties at Kincora while under police investigation.

16
FACE TO FACE

It was St Valentine's Day 1990. The wind blew cold off the County Down coast and the people of Ballyhalbert huddled by their firesides for warmth. Smoke billowed from virtually every chimney and the sea lashed against the rocks as I drove along the main street that hugged the shoreline. My mission? To find William McGrath and pursue the truth. In the nine years in which I had been investigating Kincora I had never before attempted to confront him, preferring instead to request interviews through members of his family or by writing to him when he was in prison. Even when he was released in December 1983 it was his son Worthington I approached at the Belfast city centre store where he worked. But now I felt I had good reason to call unannounced. A new controversy was about to propel the Kincora affair into the news again. This time the subject was of an extremely serious nature as it concerned MI5's success in blocking a police investigation into the affair – or so I had been told a few days earlier by a very reliable source. The Kincora trail was hot again.

Uncertain of McGrath's exact address I parked in the forecourt of a neighbourhood shop with the intention of asking if anyone could direct me to his home. I purchased a few items – a bag of potatoes, a packet of cigarettes and a bar of chocolate. Presenting them for payment I casually asked the shopkeeper if she could point me in the direction of McGrath's house. Politely, but firmly, she declined, offering me the opinion that as far as she and others in the village were concerned 'Billy' McGrath was a friendly, likeable man who said he had been badly wronged in the courts and who had been pestered by reporters. 'I suppose you are one of them,' she said bluntly. I owned up and then politely suggested that in spite of what he had to say, the police evidence which convicted him indicated that far from being wronged, McGrath had actually got off very lightly. Collecting my change, I headed out to the car to consider my next move. I could always begin the door-to-door routine but the attitude of the shopkeeper suggested that I would receive little cooperation.

Stories had been circulating that McGrath had been busy attempting to ingratiate himself with a local clergyman and had been making as yet unsuccessful attempts to regain membership of the Orange Order, going as far as to resume his correspondence with a number of politicians and suggesting that he should meet them soon to discuss the deteriorating situation in Northern Ireland. Orange Order sources had informed me that McGrath would never again be admitted into their fold, not with his reputation as a discredited liar and homosexual rapist who made no attempt to defend himself in court. I noticed an elderly man approach. He wore a cardigan, dark trousers and slippers, so obviously he did not have too far to travel. I got out of the car and watched as he moved steadily towards the shop. There is a God, I thought, as he got within range.

Gingerly I edged around the car in order to get between him and the shop door, proffering my hand as he reached me. He accepted, we shook and I announced myself as 'Chris Moore from the BBC'. He smiled wryly in recognition, as though he had been expecting me some day, and told me he had nothing to say. Don't you want to defend yourself, your good name? He replied that he had been pestered by reporters in recent times and had received six offers from newspapers for his version of the Kincora story. For the next fifteen or twenty minutes, though, he stood his ground and said quite a bit more than, I suspect, either he or I thought he might. I had never met the man before, yet strangely I felt as though I had known him for a long time. Nine years of gathering information on McGrath the enigma had created the illusion in my head that I was familiar with the man himself. It was nonsense of course, but the information I gathered was very useful indeed.

Immediately I was struck by his communication skills. For the first time I had opportunity to witness for myself the oratorical abilities which former friends and colleagues had so accurately described. It was easy to understand how he had been able to survive for so many years undetected, how he had an ability to lead his life in several different compartments at once. Above all, even though I knew how evil he could be and how he could corrupt young minds, I was amazed at how plausible he could make it all sound. Had I not known the truth about so much of his life, he might well have succeeded in persuading me of his innocence. I hung on his every word, trying to imagine him giving a talk in a room packed with Orangemen, or a church full of evangelical Christians, every now and then remembering Sammy's description of the brutal rape, the contemptuous way in which he believed he had a right to use Sammy's body. If Sammy had been there then, there would have been no conversation. But I was there to listen, to ask questions and to report what McGrath had to say to a public waiting to hear from a man I had helped to demonise by my coverage of the Kincora affair.

From the outset McGrath was adamant that he would not do an interview for television, not even on audio tape, even to attempt to have his say or clear his name. 'I have my loyalties,' he said by way of explanation as to why he would not go public. 'The truth of Kincora has not yet come out,' he said intriguingly. 'Any intelligent man can tell that,' he said, 'for in spite of all the millions of words written and spoken about it so far, no one has been told the truth. I and I alone can tell the true story of Kincora.' But no amount of persuasion could convince him to talk now. Then he hit me with it! 'If I were to tell the truth about Kincora it would be told without the use of one word ... sex! That word would not feature at all.' What about the long list of witnesses who would use the word sex? 'I am aware of that.' I have seen the statements made against you, I told him. 'So have I,' he replied. But I have spoken to some of the young men who made statements and they have told me you sexually abused them. 'If that is what you want to believe,' he responded. But why would anyone want to fit him up for criminal activities if he was not guilty? How could so many different people join together in such a conspiracy? There was no response. I pressed ahead. What about the medical report? The doctor said you were a classic example of an active homosexual?

'I know, I have seen that as well,' he said.

At this point he edged around me towards the shop. Fearing I would lose him, I said it was difficult to believe that all these people would suddenly decide to tell lies about him in some enormous conspiracy. He turned as he reached the shop door and said: 'You know, there are wheels within wheels.' I asked what he meant by that statement. 'This whole matter does not stop at Lisburn.' He turned and entered the shop. His last sight of me must have been with my mouth hanging open in amazement. 'Lisburn.' That was the significant word. Lisburn was the town where British Army Headquarters was based. It was also headquarters for operatives in various intelligence gathering agencies – for Army Intelligence, for the undercover Army Intelligence Corps – and it was one of two bases used by MI5. It was at Lisburn where James had been 'blown out' by the 'political adviser' who was actually a senior figure in MI5 and who, according to some of McGrath's loyal followers, was his handler. I waited outside, determined not to leave at this stage, I wanted to know more. No doubt the shopkeeper was telling him about my arrival and my sneaky request for assistance to help find him, and he was being offered escape through a back door for all I knew. But I waited. I was delighted, and a little surprised, when after a few minutes he stepped out again, advancing towards his home – and me.

McGrath made no attempt to avoid me and he seemed as amiable as he had been before he went into the shop, although he would not be drawn to offer further explanation on the 'Lisburn' comment. My next approach concerned Paisley. Why, I asked, was Paisley so quick to dump him when they had been so closely associated over a great many years? He denied ever having a 'close friendship with Paisley'. Had he not been involved with Paisley through his political activities? Again a denial. I pushed on. Had he and Roy Garland not gone on occasion to meet Paisley. 'I never had any personal dealings with Paisley,' he responded, adding: 'I may have met him while attending rallies when hundreds of other people were present.' Now I knew he was telling lies because of the evidence of so many others who clearly remember meetings at Paisley's church (and Garland remembered calling on at least one occasion to Paisley's house). And the delegation to Prime Minister Chichester-Clark in 1969? Now I could see McGrath's *modus operandi*. His game plan was to treat me as someone who did not know as much as I did, to use his old trick of not allowing one part of his life know about the other parts. It was time to nail down this lie. Were your children not married in Paisley's church? 'I am not a Paisleyite and never have been,' he replied, before adding: 'They were not children of mine.' But, of course, I knew they were, because I had the marriage certificates. Did your daughter Elizabeth not marry Frankie Millar in Paisley's church, I asked. He hesitated, but then said: 'Yes.' And was your son Worthington not married in that same Paisley church? Again a slight hesitation before: 'Yes. That is right.' So they are two children of yours? 'Yes.' So you did know Paisley and his church quite well? He told me the only other occasion he met Paisley, aside from the two weddings, was when he took a couple of overseas visitors to see Martyrs Memorial Church. 'I never met Paisley on political matters,' he said categorically. Had I been ignorant of the fact that his children had been married in Paisley's church, it would have been easy for McGrath to convince me of his veracity. He was obviously convinced that I did not know about another part of his life – the family man.

I tried to get back on the 'Lisburn' trail by mentioning all the recent allegations about the involvement of British Intelligence in the Kincora affair. He would not respond. I mentioned all the suggestions that he had been working for military intelligence but he was not to be drawn. I spoke about the police discovering that he had first come to the attention of MI6 back in 1958. This drew a smile, but no comment. He was on the move as I again tried to tempt him to have his say. Did he not think he was entitled to have his say? The thought, he said, had occurred to him. Then he jokingly suggested that one day he might write a book. How would it look if you were to die before you put forward your side of the story? He just smiled. As he got nearer his home, with me still on his shoulder, he expressed the hope that I would not be writing this up for a story. I informed him that I had introduced myself as a reporter for the BBC and that he had talked freely and that yes I did intend at some point to use the information in a story. I watched him walk into his home, naturally noting the address. It was about fifty yards from the shop. McGrath made his way to his front door and we said farewell.

The house, a bungalow, looked attractive and prosperous. I made a mental note to find out a little more about this. After all it was nearly ten years since McGrath had got his last wage packet – and he had moved to this new bungalow between the time of his arrest in April 1980 and his conviction in December 1981: his letter to lodge members in October 1981 was addressed from Harbour Road, Ballyhalbert, a matter of weeks before he was jailed. I discovered that the mortgage to the house was in the name of his son Harvey who lived in America. My face-to-face had all happened so quickly that it was only as I drove away I realised I had not done something which I normally do in these circumstances, I had not given McGrath a business card with my telephone numbers, in case, having thought it over, he wanted to get in touch. I turned the car and headed back, parked and knocked on the front door.

I apologised to McGrath and explained that I would like to leave my card in case he changed his mind. Surprisingly, he stopped on the doorstep for another short chat. This time he got into political speech mode, expressing the view that the world was changing, in a state of flux. Ireland, he told me, would in the next ten or fifteen years become a very different place. 'There will be big changes,' he emphasised, 'some amazing changes.' He repeated that his loyalties were to the cause he had served all his life . . . to Northern Ireland and to Ireland the island. He looked ahead to 1992 when changes in Europe would effectively remove national border restrictions. 'Listen closely to what certain politicians are saying at the moment,' he said. 'Some of them will make amazing decisions in the years ahead.' His political work, he declared, was the real reason for what he described as 'the persecution of Billy McGrath.' Then he asked: 'Why is Billy McGrath being persecuted? If I was a homosexual and if I had sex with all the boys I am supposed to have had, why persecute me? There are thousands out there in the world having homosexual relations every day and there is not a word about it. So why pick on me? Why not the scoutmaster? [This was a reference to Peter Bone, one of the six jailed in the same trial as McGrath]. Or why not Joe Mains or Raymond Semple? They have picked on me not because of who I am, but because of the cause I represent.'

I mentioned to McGrath that I had seen a document published in 1986 relating to the Anglo-Irish Agreement, which had been signed at Hillsborough in November 1985 by the British and Irish Prime Ministers. This document, I said, was printed by Tara. He admitted it was his work, and asking me to wait a moment, he went inside and returned with the document in his hand. He handed it to me as I moved back into the question of British Intelligence involvement in Kincora. Could he offer guidance as to whether there was any substance to the claims about British Intelligence? Before answering he sought an assurance [which was given] that what he was about to say would not be quoted as it would 'make me out to be a liar with the other reporters who had called'. Given that McGrath is now dead I feel I am released from my undertaking. This was the answer he gave: 'The first I knew of Kincora was when I came home one evening and the *Sunday World* was thrown down in front of me.' Given that the story broke originally in the *Irish Independent*, I was a little confused. Did he mean this was the first time a story had been written about British Intelligence and Kincora? Just when he was getting interesting, McGrath seemed suddenly to realise that he was getting drawn in too deeply and he declined to explain any further – or the movement of his wife in the hallway behind him may have had something to do with this change of mind. McGrath shifted inside and soon I was back in the car, moving slowly a short distance out of sight of the house to write up a few notes and take another look at the four-page phamplet 'Issued by the Tara Group'. I had seen it before, but now as I read it a second time I could see that it represented everything I knew to be true about McGrath. Even after his imprisonment, McGrath was clearly soon back into his old ways, with a few loyal supporters to stand by him and keep the name of Tara alive. This 1986 document on the Anglo-Irish Agreement has the feel of a self-penned epitaph and for that reason I believe it is worth reproducing in full:

THE ANGLO-IRISH AGREEMENT

It is with much dismay, and not a little apprehension, that we fail to see any mention of the part the Church of Rome has played in bringing about the Anglo-Irish Agreement. Failure to recognise her share in all this makes it impossible to correctly assess the reality of our present position and the future developments which the enemy hopes to impose upon us. What a glorious opportunity this was to name the real enemy! It goes without saying that the Anglo-Irish Agreement could not have reached its present stage without the full support and approval of the Vatican. It is impossible for the ordinary man to understand and rightly estimate the clandestine activity and influence of the Church of Rome in our national life. Perhaps the best description of this activity was that given by the late Lord Robert Montague, when he said: 'Emperors have resisted it and fallen. Ministers have framed their policies to curb the pretensions of the Pope and have been overcome. The devices of Premiers are weak, in opposition to the intrigues of the Curia. The advance of the Papacy has always been as the advance of the plague, irresistible, unsparing, remorseless, and deadly. Its myriads of secret agents overmatch armies and dispose of their generals. Its purposes are fathomless as the sea and silent as the grave. Its action is in every state, setting nation to hamper nation, and exciting one statesman against another; breaking up, dividing, crumbling its enemies; while its own party is always united, conspiring everywhere towards one object.'

The situation today in Ireland and at Westminster is no different from that prevailing at the time of the Home Rule Bill. In an article in the *St James's Gazette*, February 27, 1885 we read: 'It is easy to show ... that England has systematically used her authority in Ireland to weaken that part of the population faithful to her, by causing it to be overwhelmed by the growing multitude of its adversaries; and now the power of the British Legislature is to be employed, under the direction of the British Executive government, finally to place the loyalists of Ireland under the heel of their enemies.'

Mr Gladstone was more honest about his intentions than our present rulers, speaking at Wigan,

October 23, 1868 he said, 'Gentlemen, I look for one to this people to put down Protestant ascendency (in Ireland). It is upon that system we are banded together to make war ... we, therefore, aim at the destruction of that system of ascendency, which though it has been crippled and curtailed by former measures, yet it still does exist. It is still there, like a tall tree of noxious growth, lifting its head to heaven and darkening and poisoning the land, so far as its shadow can extend. It is still there, Gentlemen; and now at length the day has come when, as we hope, the axe has been laid at the root of that tree, and it nods and quivers from its top to its base. It wants, Gentlemen, for one stroke more ... it will then, once for all, totter to its fall; and on that day the heart of Ireland will leap for joy.' Make no mistake about it, this is not a struggle between Unionism and Republicanism – these are only necessary political labels – this is a struggle between fundamental Protestantism and Romanism for the soul of Iireland. Let the born-again Christians take note, for they, because of the glorious Gospel which they proclaim, are the main target in this confrontation.

It is undoubtedly true that many of the politicians at Westminster are so spiritually destitute that they fail to understand the nature and the outcome of the tragedy enshrined in the Anglo-Irish Agreement. Because of the ecumenical and internationalist atmosphere in which they live, it seems only a matter for ridicule to suggest that the Church of Rome has any political ambitions for the British people. Yet, her age long ambition still stands – 'To bend and to break the will of an imperial people.' This is the basis of all the thinking and the planning at the Vatican and in Dublin behind the Anglo-Irish Agreement. This Agreement is only a detail of Rome's long-term strategy for these islands, a strategy that involves the abolition of the Act of Settlement, the Romanising of the royal House, and placing the Papacy in an official place of influence and power in our national life. That is the aim if not the words of the Anglo-Irish Agreement.

We must not be deceived by the words of peace now coming from the R.C. Clergy. Their aim has not changed. Violence for them has served its purpose. Without violence the Anglo-Irish Agreement could never have been laid on the table in Hillsborough. Let no one be surprised that Rome has changed her position, she deserted her lifelong friends in Italy to sign the Concordat with Mussolini, likewise her friends in Germany to sign the Concordat with Hitler. Now she is deserting her 'hatchetmen' in Ireland in favour of her more accommodating friends at Westminster. With what results? The end of Irish neutrality/The establishment of a NATO base in Éire? British and American Warships in Southern ports? A bitter pill indeed for the 'hatchetmen'. This is the price Rome is prepared to pay in order to see the Ulster Protestant in chains! Such is the nature of the Anglo-Irish Agreement. What of the outcome for Northern Ireland? For the Ulster Protestant this

Agreement will bring great bitterness of soul. What could be worse than to be betrayed by friends? This bitterness will be reinforced by the presence of a foreign Secretariate in our midst, the emasculation of our Courts and Security Forces and no doubt, joint British/Éire Army patrols under the supervision of Common Market Officers to keep us in subjection. Along with this there will be a score of other indignities but in all this there is a glory that is supremely ours. The Ulster Protestant has been called to take his stand against what appear to be overwhelmingly impossible odds, lest the forces of rebellion and apostasy finally overrun all of the British people. Many dark and anxious days lie before us. It behoves us to be much in prayer that faith and freedom might be preserved and that wisdom and courage be given to our people at this time. Let no unworthy act besmirch the glory of the cause we serve. Let no bitterness destroy our spirit no matter what humiliation we have to endure. There will be many humiliations till God has His way with these evil men who have crept into places of authority in our land. There is one line we must never cross! Whatever humiliation we have to endure, whatever price we have to pay, we must never surrender our British citizenship and our position under the Crown! These are not negotiable under any circumstance! With renewed faith in the God of our fathers, knowing that it is better to suffer now than to be slaves for ever, let us hold Ulster, whatever the cost, that Ireland might be saved and Britain reborn.

The reason for my visit to McGrath's home was that I had just received from a very reliable source information regarding MI5's refusal to produce a key witness during the second police investigation, the one being overseen by the Chief Constable of Sussex, Sir George Terry. A BBC 2 programme, *Public Eye*, took an interest in my researches and for the next four months I worked out of their London office on a special one-hour programme on the blockage of the police enquiry. I was not permitted to use material from my conversation with McGrath in the programme, which was transmitted on 1 June 1990.

A few weeks after it had gone out I once again tried to persuade McGrath to speak publicly but this time his door was swiftly and firmly closed in my face. It was an understandable response; the programme severely damaged his credibility, for the first time broadcasting interviews with youths he had abused, including the young man he had so brutally raped, Sammy. Sammy had received a payment of a five-figure sum in compensation from the Northern Ireland authorities. It was the largest settlement agreed and that too is understandable. There is no doubt that the transmission would have made it more difficult for people to believe that McGrath was framed. It certainly blew McGrath's cover on some of the separate compartments of his life and it certainly lifted the lid on the extent of the cover-up perpetrated by MI5 to protect McGrath, who was just a small part of a larger operation.

17
MI5 Says No

There have been six enquiries into various aspects of the Kincora affair, but despite many hundreds of hours of investigation and interrogation in the decade between 1980 and 1990 these enquiries have failed to dispel public disquiet about events at the hostel – and in particular suspicions about the role of the intelligence services in the mid-1970s. The first of three RUC investigations was in 1980 and it resulted in the conviction of the three Kincora staff, Mains, Semple and McGrath. A month after these convictions the then Secretary of State James Prior announced the establishment of a Committee of Enquiry to be headed by the former Ombudsman for Northern Ireland, Stephen McGonagle. He enjoyed a reputation as a robust and thorough investigator, although in this instance he regarded his terms of reference as rather narrow in that they limited him to an examination of the administration and management of state-run homes and hostels. His committee sat for one day and heard evidence from just one witness before it collapsed in failure with the resignations of three members. They resigned following newspaper stories and my story of 12 February 1980, in which for the first time young men who had been in public care spoke about the abuses they were forced to endure. They said they had come to their decision 'because of the continuing persistent and escalating suggestion that major criminal aspects of the case are still outstanding' and did not feel able to continue until 'these matters have been satisfactorily resolved.'

The collapse of the McGonagle enquiry brought two new investigations; one headed by the Chief Constable of Sussex, Sir George Terry, was to examine whether the police had been party to a cover-up on Kincora by being negligent in the 1970s. A new RUC enquiry was to be led by Superintendent George Caskey, who had conducted the first police investigation and was supervised by Sir George Terry. Sir George completed his report in October 1983 and the following year a public enquiry got under way with retired English judge William Hughes as its chairman. His brief, however, was much the same as McGonagle's.

Once all these investigations had been completed it was possible for the British parliamentary establishment to argue that there was no further cause for public concern. Both Hughes and Terry concluded that there was no deliberate cover-up although Sir George criticised the police because there was what he described as 'several occasions when, through inadequacy or inefficiency, insufficient cognisance was taken by supervisory officers of the implications of information...' These investigations appeared to lay Kincora to rest, but a close look at the terms of reference reveals that neither report could enter the crucial area of the intelligence services' awareness of Kincora. The Terry report was never offered in full for public consumption and perhaps because of the limited terms of reference it was widely assumed that the RUC enquiry did not try to investigate the most sensitive aspects of the Kincora affair, the involvement of MI5. However, as I discovered in 1990, this was not the case. The RUC, under the leadership of Superintendent George

Caskey and the supervision of Sir George Terry, did try to probe the activities of the intelligence services. They did try to put key questions to the senior officer in MI5 who had blown James out of his office; the political adviser at Army Headquarters in Lisburn who had ordered James to leave Kincora alone and drop his source in Tara. When I was told this my mind went back to 1982, a time the second police investigation was in progress.

I received a telephone call from a very well informed source at my home one Sunday evening, requesting an immediate meeting in a shopping centre car park near both our houses. As I sat in the darkness of his car he told me that it was London, Whitehall to be precise, that was really nervous of this investigation, not anyone in Northern Ireland. He could not be specific but he urged me to concentrate my efforts on the other side of the water where, he said, there was extreme unease about the whole Kincora affair and especially about this second investigation. My difficulty was that the information was so general I could not find a means of identifying the line to follow and my network of contacts at that stage did not offer the kind of insight I needed into what was a politically sensitive investigation. In short, the opportunity was lost on me at the time but now in 1990 I was getting a second chance. This time I had the backing of a BBC network programme and all the resources it could muster for such an important story.

Once I had passed on my information about the blockage of the RUC and Sir George Terry's investigation, I was taken on board the *Public Eye* team and a series of meetings with senior BBC executives followed as we plotted our course. These were often attended by John Birt, the new head of news and current affairs. Everything was checked and double-checked. For example, when we traced James and heard first-hand his story about being dressed down by MI5 when he reported McGrath's homosexuality and pederasty, we carefully checked out his story. I was tasked to make contact with a local family in County Down who, according to James, had been friends of his through their activities together in a Christian group. Everything tallied, so by this and a number of other checks on his army background we were assured of the reliability of James.

When Caskey's team had made contact with James, naturally they also wanted access to the MI5 man who prevented James from passing on to police the details he had discovered from his Tara source. We traced him to a house in the Greater London commuter area. BBC reporter Peter Taylor visited him and I spoke to him by telephone. He hung up on me. He told Taylor he had no idea the RUC wanted to question him and he said he could not clearly recall the meeting with James, although he did not deny he had met the man. The RUC's requests for access to him for questioning were rejected. They wanted to know why he had not reported James's findings to the police. But where do police officers wishing to contact an MI5 man begin? In this case, they began with a visit to Stormont, where the Northern Ireland Office is based. This was their starting point because this man was in charge of MI5 operations in Northern Ireland although his exact title, as we know, was 'political adviser.' They met a deputy secretary who – as it happened – had been recently attached to the Ministry of Defence. His name was John Bourne.

The RUC detectives were directed to the Ministry of Defence offices at Whitehall. Several meetings took place there between the RUC and an official from the Ministry of Defence, but in spite of repeated requests the political adviser was never made available for interview. No explanation was ever given. In Whitehall, RUC detectives met a senior official by the name of Groat as the first point of contact. He did not make it any easier for them to unravel who was Military Intelligence, who was security services. In Northern Ireland, Military Intelligence and MI5 work closely together and it was important for the police from Belfast to try to establish who was responsible for who. But given the extreme rivalry and mistrust between the RUC and MI5, perhaps there was never much likelihood of the Northern Irish police making much headway at MOD headquarters in London. In sheer frustration, further approaches were made through the Northern Ireland Office, and the next step was a compromise: the RUC would submit a series of questions in writing. The list included the following:

1 Why no action was taken to investigate the allegations James had passed on?
2 Why James was told to 'drop' Kincora?
3 Why he was told to sever contact with his source?
4 Did MI5 know what was going on in the home?
5 If MI5 did know, was it prepared to let it continue for another purpose?

No answers were ever received and the police enquiry came to a halt. Of course, there may be another explanation: that MI5 was already feeling extremely sensitive given that Northern Ireland's security coordinator Sir Maurice Oldfield had been compelled during his short stay in Belfast (1979-80) to confess that he was himself homosexual. While preparing the *Public Eye* story, Peter Taylor, an experienced reporter and commentator on Irish affairs, used his own contacts to try to establish from MI5 some kind of rationale for the refusal to release the political adviser for questioning by the RUC. The final section of the programme described the outcome of these enquiries, explaining that the government was firmly against any further enquiry and quoting the Northern Ireland Secretary Peter Brooke: 'The Kincora affair has been investigated as fully and thoroughly as lies within the power of the government to investigate it.' This is what Taylor reported:

> So on what grounds do the authorities base that conviction? After long and detailed enquiries that started many weeks ago, this is what I was finally told yesterday. First: that the RUC did express an interest in interviewing the MI5 officer – although the view was taken that he was never central to their investigation. Enquiries made by the appropriate authorities elicited that the officer concerned had no specific information that was relevant to the enquiry in hand – and the interview was not pursued by the RUC This was because, according to the authorities, he had nothing significant to say about

Kincora and therefore had nothing to say at any interview. Second: if he had had something relevant to say, there was no specific operational or source protection requirement to prevent him speaking to the police. Third: there was general concern that had the MI5 officer been spoken to, any line of police questioning would be likely to reveal matters connected with the structure, organisation and *modus operandi* of intelligence agencies. So it would appear that although the RUC's questions were simple and specific – and, according to what I [Taylor] have been told – could have been dealt with ... they were not answered in order to safeguard the operations of the security service. This raises a fundamental question of accountability.

Indeed it does. Furthermore, it means that, unlike us ordinary citizens, the British establishment's intelligence services can, if it suits, refuse to answer questions put by those employed by the state to prevent and investigate crime. They can adopt this attitude even if it implies that they regard the integrity and security of the state as being above all else, including the law, including the sexual abuse of young men in public care facing attacks by an agent of those same security services. In short, the 'political adviser' protected McGrath – and the security services protected the political adviser from questioning by the RUC. After the BBC programme I returned to Belfast – and that, as they say, would have been that ... except ...

Back into the old routine in Belfast, I was enjoying a few pints with mates when someone approached me seeking a 'quiet word'. It was a senior civil servant who from time to time in the past had helped me with information, a useful contact and a person I could trust. This individual said there was much more to the Kincora story than had been revealed in the statement supplied to Taylor, that there had been a long-running MI5 operation centred on Kincora and with McGrath an active agent of the intelligence agency. There was a code word for the operation; and my source knew someone who had greater knowledge of the affair and who might be persuaded to help; I should leave the contact to him. A bad move, as it happens, because my contact did himself no favours by making the approach to this other party. In fact, there was a dressing down from a person who appeared to have intelligence agency connections with a warning that they knew everything the BBC had [this I took to be a reference to my work on the Kincora affair] and that if care was not taken people might just find themselves getting their fingers burned, maybe even ending up inside the Maze Prison like others who had become too inquisitive about Kincora. Was I being warned off? I took it that I was.

For the next few years Kincora was placed on the back burner. The information dried up for a time, as it had in the past, and I set off for Manchester for a few years to watch United win their first Premier League title. But I knew Kincora would eventually get a fresh kick into life. It did, quite by chance, in 1993, when I met Adrian. This was enough to put me on the trail again and that in turn resulted in a meeting in England with one of the Tara mid-1970s group. He in turn led me to meet another member of the group from the same era. Now it was this man, let us call him Alf, who met me at the Sprucefield roundabout on the M1 just before midnight one Wednesday night. I was familiar with his name because of my enquiries in 1982 and had even met him during a house call when I was looking for someone else, although at the time I could only guess at his identity.

Parked at Sprucefield, Alf and I talked for an hour or so about his experience of working in Tara with McGrath. From the outset he made it clear that some members of Tara were not entirely convinced of McGrath's guilt, although he personally did not express an opinion one way or the other on this matter. He did say that there was a small number of individuals who were keeping the name of Tara alive by continuing the work begun by McGrath many years before. In their view Tara was little more than an information-gathering instrument for the British intelligence network. Alf put forward the theory that McGrath became surplus to requirements when there was a change in British government policy away from total integration for Northern Ireland within the British Constitution towards what he and his friends perceived as a more neutral position – if not a leaning towards a united Ireland. He linked this change in government policy to Sir Maurice Oldfield's removal from the security services in Northern Ireland and referred to McGrath's case on one occasion as the 'greatest political frame-up ever', which prevented McGrath from fulfilling his true potential.

One remark Alf made which really grabbed my attention was his claim that McGrath and the 'political adviser' knew each other. Whether or not they did, there is no doubt that the political adviser's decision to put a block on an Army Intelligence officer from learning more about McGrath and Kincora prevented the information from being passed on to the police ... and as we now know there was a reason for wishing to keep the lid on Kincora. There has never been an enquiry into the political associations of McGrath, to determine just who in British Intelligence knew what about Tara, McGrath and his nefarious activities. Those who suffered in Kincora for the sake of a security operation deserve to hear the truth. They should not be regarded as expendable in order to protect those in authority who knew what was going on but did nothing. Those charged with protecting the integrity of the state should be accountable for their actions and the government owes it to those abused in Kincora to make them accountable. In reality, there's more chance of my playing for Manchester United before the end of the current season ...

Afterword

Everyone in Northern Ireland – people of all religions and people of none – has suffered through the twenty-seven years of bloody conflict, whether bereavement, injury, the loss of a job or an insult from strangers in a bar in Spain. All have had their lives curtailed, their horizons dimmed.

For too many the suffering has been so intense that the human heart can hardly cope with it. Against the background of that grief and pain, the grim and mysterious figure of William McGrath is not just an enigma but an irony.

Here was a man who lived in the shadows, who shunned the light of day, who told his closest associates that he preferred to 'remain a backroom boy'. Layers of meaning were concealed by that sly remark. McGrath lived a secret and perverted homosexual life for years but he was also in contact with the impenetrable world of secret intelligence. McGrath was told things; McGrath knew things. It is clear that McGrath knew too much because he knew in advance – if only in outline – that the conflict was coming.

This was long before the debauched days of Kincora. The quest for the truth has centred on what happened and how things happened between the late 1960s, when McGrath set up Tara, and 1980, when the abuse of boys in a hostel in East Belfast was disclosed. The whole truth is still denied us; some of those who might enlighten us remain under protection in the secret places of Whitehall.

In the years from 1969 to 1980 reactionary loyalist paramilitarism and the IRA and other groups in the vanguard of republicanism turned Northern Ireland into a cockpit of terror. Loyalist paramilitarism owed much to the machinations of William McGrath, much more than rank and file loyalists could ever have imagined. Soon after the first terrorist murders of the new-style UVF, Tara acted as a catalyst providing recruits both for it and for the emerging UDA. McGrath was the author of what other writers have called the 'birth certificate' of the UDA.

Apparently, McGrath did not initiate the 'Tara brigade', as he liked to call it. As Billy told me once:

> With the benefit of hindsight I believe that Tara was essentially set up, funded and indeed organised by the British security service, MI5. For a start, finance never seemed to be a problem, then there was McGrath's talent for predicting events long before they ever came about and of course what he told us about people of influence and the intelligence community. I believe Tara was effectively the property of MI5, was in fact a safety net – used to control paramilitary elements within the loyalist group in the event of a total breakdown of law and order.

McGrath made it obvious to all those who heard him speak that he was acting on intelligence. There was a higher authority; McGrath was not alone. Figures like John McKeague spring to mind, and there are other documented episodes like the Colin Wallace affair and the case of Brian Nelson to suggest strongly that British Intelligence had penetrated and was manipulating the loyalist paramilitary underground from the early 1970s onwards. Where was the democratic control over all this unquestionably illegal activity? Why have elected representatives, including MPs from Northern Ireland itself, been so reluctant to become involved in uncovering the truth?

McGrath drew the attention of some of those closest to him to an emerging pattern in the street violence in the early days of the conflict: a pattern that was to have a profound effect on the thinking of the British public. Republican street agitation would subside, only to be replaced by a fierce outburst on the part of loyalists burning buses and stoning the police, for instance on Belfast's Protestant Shankill Road. McGrath argued that this spiral of violence in which terrorist and counter-terrorist alike attacked the security forces while striving to get at each other's throats – the infamous 'tit-for-tat' equation – was no accident.

The psychological impact of these disorders on British public opinion was to have an important political consequence. Seeing the security forces caught, pig-like, in the middle sapped any commitment there might have been to the resolution of the conflict in Northern Ireland. Disenchantment and cynicism about the province's 'tribal conflict' created a climate in which the London establishment could push forward policies, safe in the knowledge that they would never be subjected to critical scrutiny at Westminster. The bipartisan approach which dominated parliamentary debate ensured that evidence of British misgovernment would be covered up. Occurrences like Kincora existed within what was effectively a quarantine zone. The British parliamentary system normally charged with protecting the interests of the ordinary voter was put into suspension. Northern Ireland offered a special set of circumstances. New rules applied, and the democratic rights of Northern Ireland Catholics and Protestants alike were ignored by British public opinion. The Kincora affair raises the very real possibility that psychological operations – psych-ops as they are termed by the military – set in train a series of events that alienated public opinion from the bloody situation in Northern Ireland. Once this had happened the establishment could cut whatever deals it thought expedient with political forces in Ireland.

So often throughout years of conflict in Northern Ireland the British government has been represented as a neutral or fair-minded umpire, detached, non-partisan and unselfish in its search for a solution.

Yet, I believe, this book presents sobering evidence that ordinary people in Northern Ireland, Protestant and Catholic alike, were goaded into actions that inflamed the tribal warfare. It is my belief that we have to ask ourselves whether William McGrath was in reality an *agent provocateur*.

Although Northern Ireland is viewed as a sectarian battleground, the extent to which disorder has been initiated by powerful agencies outside the state has often gone unnoticed. This book indicates that the emotions and passions of ordinary working people are open to manipulation.

In the nature of things it cannot be conclusively proven that McGrath was an agent of British Intelligence. However, the events of the past three decades are well documented and, given the incalculable sums of money poured by the

British Exchequer into the crucible of Northern Ireland, the constant appearance of the conflict at the lower end of the opinion polls points up the abandonment of the issue by the British public. In an age of media manipulation and spin doctors, this reaction by public opinion could hardly have been entirely accidental.

It is not, of course, argued that the Kincora sex scandal alone carries responsibility for this. The contention of this book is that in the story of William McGrath we get a glimpse of how Britain's secret state tried to control and direct events in Northern Ireland. I hope that the story which this book develops has uncovered a number of pieces in a large jigsaw. In the interlocking pattern we see a scenario begin to emerge. Many other pieces are resistant to being explored, understood and assembled.

William McGrath remains inscrutable to this day. Despite the statements of many witnesses and the medical evidence, he did not break under police interrogation. After his release from prison he still circulated occasional letters, written in the same evengelical and prophetic style as earlier documents. Nothing had changed. He neither repented nor recanted. He maintained a rigorous silence about his past. An intelligence operative who played a pivotal role in bringing McGrath's dark past into the light of day brought his interview with this author to a close with this enigmatic question: 'Is it possible that in the case of William McGrath we are dealing with a trained mind?'

In this book is presented the fruit of intensive research, I trust in the form of fresh insights that will provoke many questions. Readers will have to decide for themselves, on the basis of the evidence presented, what was the true nature of the life and role of William McGrath ... at least until the next piece of evidence presents himself for public scrutiny.

APPENDIX
TARA PROCLAMATION

On the following pages is the text of the Tara Proclamation which Adrian (Chapter 9) read in the Belfast *News Letter* of 20 June 1974. These pages are reproduced in facsimile from a Tara publication.

TARA PROCLAMATION

BEING CONVINCED that darker days than we have yet known still lie ahead for the people of Northern Ireland, we address ourselves to those who wish to preserve for ALL THE PEOPLE OF IRELAND, that heritage of faith and freedom that has been almost extinguished in a large part of our land and which is now threatened with extinction in the North-East corner of Ulster.

The aim of the enemy is the destruction of our Protestant faith. This they hope to achieve by creating a total war situation in which the Eire Army will cross the Border to unite with the Provisional and Regular I.R.A. who are already in our midst. Plans are in existence for this purpose. What has happened in our Province during the past few years is not just a series of local riot situations, but rather the beginning of the final chapter of an age-long campaign to subjugate and subdue the Protestant people of Ireland. This is an essential preparation for the campaign against the Protestant character of the British Throne. This situation will continue to grow in intensity until the final battle which will affect the life of every man and woman, boy and girl in our land. For such a conflict our Protestant people are ill-prepared. In preparation for the day of battle certain things are essential NOW.

(1) Our Protestant districts must be brought back to normality in the shortest possible time. Damage must be repaired. The whole place cleaned up. Every home, shop, office, factory and street must be bright and shining. showing to the world that Protestantism stands for, at least, cleanliness and order and industrious living.

(2) Our children must be sent to Sunday School and Church. If your Minister is not a true Protestant get him moved and put a man of God in his place. These men are paid to preach the Protestant faith in its purity. Don't let them take their money under false pretences. It is not sufficient that your children have been born Protestant, they must be taught the fundementals of their faith. There are many good Mission Halls which should be supported by you and your family, Learn to raise your heart in prayer to God through Christ, at your Bench, Desk or in the Bus, the Car or the Home. The people that pray are an invinceable people.

(3) Law and Order must prevail. Hi-jacking, Robbery, Illegal Drinking Clubs and an utter disregard for other people's

property are no part of the Protestant way of life. People who indulge in these activities must be exposed for the criminals that they are.

(4) Victimisation and intimidation must stop. It serves no cause to burn a man's home or destroy his place of work. Each person must be allowed to live and work in peace and security in keeping with the dignity of man.

(5) Assassination must stop. Many of the victims have not been politically active. Their death had no political significance or effect. Capital punishment must be the penalty for murder.

(6) If the spirit of rebellion arises in an individual or a community, all the strength of the Lawful Authorities must be used to crush it without mercy.

(7) Maximum co-operation and support must at all times be given to the Army and Poilce. If wrong political directions are given to the Security Forces resulting in unacceptable action by them, we must do everything possible to cool the situation. The only time we would oppoşe the Security Forces would be in the event of them forcing us into a United Ireland. If we act now and act righlty this situation will never arise. It is our task to educate the Forces as to the nature of the conflict and the rightness of our cause, so that in the final battle the Army and Police will be fighting side by side with us against a common foe, namely Romanism and Communism.

(8) We must campaign now for integrated education. All Roman Catholic centres of education must be closed. Religious education must be provided only by Evangelical Protestants.

(9) The Roman Catholic Church must be declared an illegal organisation. History proves that it is a conspiracy against the fortunes and liberties of mankind. For generations this evil thing has blighted our land. It must be destroyed, so that our fellow countrymen who have been deceived by it, will have an opportunity of entering into an eternal relationship with God through Christ and of discovering their common identity with us. The indivisble oneness of the Irish people will then become a reality.

twenty-eight

(10) Conflict is inevitable. We would not choose this path but the forces of Romanism and Communism will. It is imperative therefore that every Protestant should be prepared to bear arms so that all our resources may be in a state of readiness to be placed under the command of the proper Authorities in the hour of need. We are not looking for trigger-happy Gunmen but we are anxious to meet responsible men who are prepared to defend their hearth and home and the glorious liberty that has come to us in the Gospel of our Lord Jesus Christ.

A basic knowledge of Guns and Ballistics of Fieldcraft and Strategy can be aquired quite legally in the privacy of one's home from books available in Public Libraries or which can be legally bought. This basic knowledge will make it possible for the great mass of law-abiding Protestants to be quickly absorbed into Her Majesty's Forces as the crises develops. Many of our people can of course find a place now in the U.D.R., or Police Reserve.

We need men of conviction, men of high principle, men of courage and of faith who are prepared to resist to the death if necessary, every attempt from whatever source, to unfurl the banner of the Evil One over this fair Province of ours.

The situation is dark. The enemy is strong, great and grievous difficulties will have to be faced, but all is not lost! Ulster is God's anvil on which is being forged the future not only of Ireland, but of all the British people of which we are proud to form a part. Knowing this, we throw down the challenge to a desperate foe — hammer away, ye hostile bands, your hammers break, God's anvil stands!

FIVE OF YOU SHALL CHASE AN HUNDRED AND AN HUNDRED OF YOU SHALL PUT TEN THOUSAND TO FLIGHT: AND YOUR ENEMIES SHALL FALL BEFORE YOU BY THE SWORD . . . FOR I WILL ESTABLISH MY CONVENANT WITH YOU . . . AND I WILL CUT OFF THE NAMES OF THE IDOLS OUT OF THE LAND AND THEY SHALL NO MORE BE REMEMBERED . . . FOR THE MOUTH OF THE LORD HATH SPOKEN IT.